OPENING

A PERSONAL STORY OF MEDIUMSHIP, GRIEF AND FAMILY HEALING

ASHLEY TYMS

 FriesenPress

One Printers Way
Altona, MB R0G 0B0
Canada

www.friesenpress.com

Edited by Joelle and Erin

ISBN
978-1-03-914870-3 (Hardcover)
978-1-03-914869-7 (Paperback)
978-1-03-914871-0 (eBook)

1. BIOGRAPHY & AUTOBIOGRAPHY, PERSONAL MEMOIRS

Distributed to the trade by The Ingram Book Company

OPENING

To all those who walk brave lives, masking the pain
or shame of mental health and addictions:
You are worthy of support and love.

To all my family and friends whose lives
were touched by our family:
You mean the world to me.

To my husband:
I cherish your support and endless love.
This wouldn't have been possible without you.

To my children, who help me learn and grow every day:
Thank you. You're incredible beings.

To my parents, whose heart and souls have
weaved into the spirit of my life:
I love you.

To Paul & Ryan:
May we always remember to be "humble and kind."

Prologue: It's Time, Ashley

Many years passed before I took this leap to complete the chapters of this book and invest in publishing.

I tuned in one day and heard Ryan say: *"It's time, Ashley."* So here we are, six years later.

My intention for this book is to honor my brothers, my family, and open my heart to heal through this story so that it may be of service to others. I share parts of our lives, and the experiences that changed mine and guided our family's healing story. I must note that both my brothers suffered many years from addiction. This topic is impactful and painful, so I will leave out those details in respect to my family. Thank you for understanding.

Each of our lives truly matters. They ripple out to more people than you can imagine. We come here to experience, to grow, to feel, to fall and choose the lessons we receive.

I invite you into the journey of my family's story.

I trust that the parts that I do share will land with you somehow. Maybe even have influence. But if not, no sweat; pass it on to another. A stranger you feel called to, or someone who could use knowing they are not alone on this Earth or beyond when they leave. We each find the missing pieces we are looking for when we are ready and open to listen and receive them.

Some of us have a different kind of sensitivity. It can be a beautiful thing, and it is something I have come to embrace and continue to learn how to care for as I grow. It is something my brother Ryan was beginning to figure out, too. My brother Paul, who also died, was much more guarded. He needed to keep himself protected, but he too had an incredible feeling heart that many counted on, while he also dreamt like a healer.

It is a great wonder that pain and death can bring you closer to yourself, Spirit, God, Allah, Source, Creator, whatever essence that connects with you. For this personal story, I owe a whole lot to my brothers. Their lives changed all of ours in huge ways.

You should know that I am an intuitive from a generational line on my father's side, and I identify as a highly sensitive Empath. I can see, feel, and sense the emotions and energies of others, places, and things, as well as those who have passed. Although I have many years' experiencing Mediumship encounters, this is not my chosen work this time around the sun.

On occasion, I help young people understand certain encounters and what helps them and Spirits. In certain unique situations, there may be a Spirit messenger that comes through in intuitive Reiki sessions, but I have a firm boundary it must only be in sessions and very clear and simple to deliver.

Currently, I own a personal practice that brings my skills as a Child & Youth Counselor together with intuitive Reiki Healing. Through Reiki training, mindful practices and healing professionals, I have healed many layers of myself and crafted my abilities over the last fifteen years. I facilitate healing light channels and intuitive insights that encourage growth while safely exploring inner and outer layers of people's energy fields and bodies. I am deeply passionate about collaborating with adults and young people to help guide them towards their inner healer. I've spent the better part of my life honing these skills.

As this book evolved into writing more about myself, I unconsciously tried to avoid it. I was asked to open my heart and myself to share the depths of my sensitivities in this book, which felt incredibly vulnerable and shaky. In the background of my mind I thought, 'Well, this leaves me open to judgment from others'. 'I need to dig deeper within myself. I do that enough already'. 'This book was supposed to be about Ryan and what happened after he died.' It felt "out there" already.

I realized people are going to judge anyway; that's what human egos do. I reflected and realized perhaps some may relate and feel less alone in reading this story. I too can judge, and it's been my personal mission over the last fifteen years to catch when I do and redirect it to prayer, to see myself in its reflection, or find the good.

I grew up in Ontario, Canada, in an old town neighborhood with lots of children in the area. My mom babysat my two best friends growing up before and after school. We spent most of our time outside playing games and make-believe. My school was six or seven blocks away; we rode a bus and later walked. My family spent a lot of weekends driving two hours to our family's cottage in Dorset, surrounded by diverse trees, animals, and beautiful Raven Lake. The cottage was usually filled with family and friends and good times. I was around many different adults growing up, so I had a keen sense of the grown-up world. Often, I got lost in the woods by myself and played with my young brother and friends up the road.

My parents were very hard workers, which gave us many opportunities. I want to acknowledge and celebrate them: thank you both so much for everything, even some of the harder stuff too! You mean so much to me and I feel truly blessed to have learned and been loved by you both. My mom completed eleven years of university from home, and my dad had a full-time job at General Motors and part time side-business, along with renters in the basement. We did a lot on our own and most of the time played outside with neighbors, friends or visited family with my father while my mom studied. My mom would take the train into Toronto early so she could travel on foot between classes to save money. Most years growing up she was in the kitchen preparing meals or sitting at the table reading or writing essays. When she completed school, she became an uncertified supply teacher, and later went to teacher's college. She was then hired full-time and was heavily involved in teaching. She was such a passionate, caring teacher and transformed many students' lives.

Ryan and I grew up very close; we were best friends. With some space in between high school and college, we came together strong at the end as well. Ryan died September 5, 2016, right before the beginning of school. Throughout this book, I share connections he made after death, how he died, parts of his life and mine growing up, and the pieces we put together that led us to experience profound family healing through grief.

When I first began writing this book, I attended a silent retreat with my mom two years after Ryan died. The quiet reflective space really helped me begin the process of remembering, feeling, and healing through writing. It took years to write because I processed the grief at deeper levels and revisited the past with curiosity, while organizing it all into words.

At my second silent retreat a year ago, I began writing a chapter about myself that was uncomfortable. With commitment and courage, I opened my heart to let others into my world, and my personal grief journey. So much good came from that.

I chose to call this book *Opening* for that reason; it offers a bird's eye view into the greater lessons of loss, while slowly opening each of our hearts to mend, heal, and come together strong.

May you read this story with an open mind, heart, and soul. Let there be space to imagine, expand, and explore what's here for you. I encourage you to dream beyond what you know or let go of what you already know to allow for possibility to come through you.

From my heart to yours, may you always be faithful to the most important person: YOU!

1: Ryan's Transcendence

2016

It all started with a phone call from our father. His voice was short and his breath shallow.

"Do you have the daycare kids at the house?" I had a home daycare business in the studio space of my home, which used to be a garage that was converted into a living space. It was a calm, colorful, and bright space with two big patio doors letting in tons of light. There was a set of stairs that led into the basement covered by a half-wall.

"No, just mine. Why?" I said.

"I need you to get to our house as soon as you can. Can I come to pick you guys up?"

With the urgent tone of his voice, I knew something was wrong.

"What's going on? Is everything okay?" I asked.

"No, not really; you just need to get here as soon as you can."

"Okay, Brandon is off work and home in about forty-five minutes; we will come right over," I said.

He ended with, "Hurry, Ashley," and hung up the phone.

Brandon worked as a bus operator for the region we live in. I was often with the kids on my own most of the time. Brandon and I dated each other for three years in our late teens; he's two years older than me. We split up for six years and found our way back to each other, married, and had two boys. He's known my family for a very long time.

Now you can only imagine everything that went through my mind after this phone call.

An array of feelings ran through me. First, anger and annoyance with my dad for not telling me what happened; second, confusion. What could it have been? I felt waves of anxiety waiting the next forty-five minutes out. I also understood the need to be in person to receive such news.

I called my husband right away. I then took my kids to the neighbors to have a short swim before Brandon got home to drive us over. In my family, we are open about things going on. I warned the kids that we got a call from Grandpa that something serious had happened and we would need to leave right away when Dad got home to find out what it was.

My youngest son, about three years old, made leaving the pool very difficult, with tears and all. With persistence and patience, we got back home to dress, got into the van, and off we went.

I remember the drive to my parents like it was yesterday. My husband asked me, "What do you think happened? Who could it be about?"

I thought and then shared out loud, "It could only be my Nanny? Papa? Or…Ryan."

I remembered that Ryan had gone up to the cottage with his girlfriend that Sunday, and this was now Monday afternoon. At that moment, something happened. It came over me like a blow to the heart, like I knew it was Ryan. I struggled to stay calm until we got there to find out.

I had lived in Whitby Ontario, at my parents' house since I was four years old. The memories and experiences run deep in my mind and heart. My husband parked on the side of the road; we pulled up to find an OPP car parked in front of the house. My aunt and uncle stood solemnly on the porch as my parents came out from the wooden screened door.

I burst out of the van quite fast before it was in park, and the police officer began approaching me. My body reacted right away; I slowed my walking and felt caution before moving. It was not the first-time the police had been to our home, as a couple of unfortunate things had happened before with my brother.

My dad walked past them slowly with his head down to the front tree by the street. My nerves created a wave of fight freeze response; I asked the police: "Can I see my dad first?"

They said, "Of course."

One of the OPP officers walked over to Brandon, who was protecting the kids' ears with the doors shut and notified him of Ryan.

I walked up to my dad, hugged him, and with a choked breath and tears in his eyes, he said, "It's Ryan, he's gone. He is at the hospital in Minden."

I was confused as I thought, *'He's at the hospital?'*

I asked, "Is he okay? Can we see him?"

Dad confirmed: "He's gone, Ashley."

It doesn't matter how many times I read this part of the chapter or revisit it all so many years later. It still hurts like it was yesterday and can drop me to my knees into full tears.

Like a shot to the chest, I fell to the ground, sobbing and crying out loud. I felt my hands and head on the ground and felt like the earth just took my body and tears and held me.

Overcome with grief, I turned and looked at my van; my two young boys and husband stood with my dad. He had informed them of my brother's death; I was in shock.

Crying, I went to my mom and held her. Together, we were in complete shock at what had happened.

At that moment, I began orienting myself. I became aware that my father was talking to my boys; my aunt and uncle were in tears watching the deliverance of the news, grief-stricken. My grandparents were there and appeared lost and in disbelief, too.

The OPP officers approached the van and gave the boys two small black DRPS teddy bears, which comforted my oldest in the year ahead. As the boys came out from the vehicle, my father asked if I wanted to go with him and my mother to see my brother's body at the hospital, but I had to decide quickly; they were leaving within ten minutes.

In complete shock with no control over my body or the news just delivered, I looked beside one of the vehicles parked in the driveway.

There he was, Ryan.

I saw his spirit body in the driveway looking at me with a facial expression of complete shock himself.

What happened? he asked me.

Seeing spirits and hearing them talking was nothing new to me, as it had been happening since I was a young girl. Seeing my brother in our home driveway asking what happened sure was new to me.

Shocked to see him, I couldn't bear to tell him he was dead.

My oldest son, who was five at the time, then approached me in tears. I got pulled back into motherhood while Ryan's presence continued to stand in the driveway as I comforted my son with a long hug.

Once my attention turned to my son and I pretended like I didn't just see Ryan, his presence disappeared for a short time.

My husband was in the doorway of the house watching me with our son, when my father asked if I decided to go or not. Brandon thought that I shouldn't go yet; I needed to stay and support the kids, who were very upset. My father thought I needed to go to be there for my mother. I felt pulled in two directions; with a heavy heart, I went within and felt the pull to be there for my parents. I also needed to see Ryan in the flesh myself.

My five-year-old son was very close to Ryan and was heartbroken too; overwhelmed with emotions. I told him he was safe, and that Mommy needed to be with Nana and Grandpa. Thankfully, our family is very close; I knew the kids would be well taken care of with Daddy, Great Grandparents, and Great Aunt and Uncle there too. Little did I know how much that moment would impact my son in the years that followed.

I quickly went to the bathroom inside my parent's house, where my brother had also been living. In the bathroom, there he appeared again; he stood close to the doorway. I heard him ask me, *What happened, Ashley?*

I laughed with tears and couldn't wrap my head around it. I still couldn't come up with a way to tell him he was gone.

A close neighbor friend drove my parent's car. I shared the back seat with my mother, Dad in the front; we were off on what felt like the longest drive of our lives. Two hours felt like eternity.

I am a mother of two boys and being at my own mother's side when she just found out she lost her son in an accident was something I wouldn't wish upon anyone. She felt numb, like part of her was dying too. We gave life to our children; of course, she felt an empty hole.

There we were, driving along a small highway discussing family members that we needed to call. I took the job. Being on the delivery end to loved ones felt complex.

I allowed tears to fall and moments of silence to flow through me before I got the courage to call anyone. Then I got pulled to look out the window.

There in my mind's eye, I saw my brother's face in the air beside the car. If you have seen the movie *Ghost* where you see the character hovering around his dead body, it was like that, but more translucent.

Ryan's face looked stunned. Then I felt an empathic feeling of that same emotion.

I felt his expression in my own body. It came in like a giant wave and crashed into my body with no control. It felt like shock, as Ryan must have realized himself that he was dead.

Then he disappeared, all in about three minutes.

I watched my father in the front of the vehicle, taking moments of gut-wrenching tears and much silence as I'm sure so many thoughts and feelings ran through him. He had lost his son. Due to my parents' reactions, I decided to stay silent about what I was witnessing from Ryan.

When I was young, I often witnessed my parents through emotionally challenging times. Raising a family can be a tough job, especially if you have unhealed parts of the past you carry with you into parenting. I believe I learned to keep certain things to myself so that I wouldn't overwhelm my parents further. As a young girl I was hyper aware of my dad's discomfort talking about spirits, and my mom didn't open any conversations about it either.

In the car I felt doubtful, conflicted but compassionate towards their feelings, so I chose not to add anything more.

Ten minutes later, there he was again in my mind's eye. I saw him fade in from the sky and trees, on the same side of the vehicle as before. This time his face had a wide-open mouth. I felt disbelief and a pause came through my body after seeing him.

Then he asked me, *promise to take care of Monica.*

Monica was my brother's girlfriend, but he was a very private man; after courting for two years, they had been officially dating for about six months, and he had not yet been ready to introduce her to the family.

Monica was religious and Ryan was shy; the long courting as friends offered them time to grow a loving connection that became a serious relationship. It would be the first time we met Monica at the hospital.

I promised Ryan at that moment that I would take care of her, and as a family, we kept that promise.

I asked my mom for Monica's phone number, and I called her cell phone, as she was at the hospital waiting. It was a bizarre feeling, calling and hearing her voice for the first time. She was so upset; I could feel her shaking body in my own as we spoke. She had the sweetest voice, and her essence was that of a rose petal. I asked her to stay there and wait for us as we were on our way. She was not alone; her best friend and another friend comforted and stayed with her.

I followed with a call to my two older half-brothers, Paul and Peter; I left them messages. We have the same dad, different moms. I called my other aunt on my mother's side, and she went into planning mode to get organized to stay the week with my mom. I called two of my best friends who were very close to my brother; they were like sisters and helped me process the news further.

There he was again! That time in my mind's eye, I saw him with his hand on his forehead and I felt sheer disappointment, like he couldn't believe this had happened. Then he disappeared into thin air. His life had many twists, turns, and serious challenges, even near-death moments. The last couple of years were picking up positive momentum; why now?

Another short five minutes went by, and I saw him again. This time his hands were hitting his head as he banged them back and forth from side to side. The energy I felt was furious; and angry as he processed all that slipped away from him.

What had happened, I wondered? I felt too overwhelmed to ask and thought he was clearly struggling with the news, so why press him more.

While the imprints and feelings took place in my body, I wondered if telling my mother was a good idea. It would be new for my mom and I to communicate openly about my contact with Spirits, what I saw and what I felt.

She continued to share her numbness and how bad she felt that she couldn't even cry. Shock can do incredible things to you, and her freeze response was strong. I witnessed her in survival mode; it was trying to protect her from the grief.

Then, minutes after she was sharing with me, I witnessed in my mind's eye what appeared to be a beige-colored hollow body. It rose above the vehicle and dropped right in between my mother and me. I heard my brother's voice say, *I'm here to comfort Mom, tell her.* His directive helped me have courage to tell her. Seeing her in pain like that made me think maybe it would help her to know he was contacting us.

I said, "Mom, Ryan is here in the car and wants to comfort you."

"Really?" she responded.

"Yes, I see a hallow golden-brown body that slid right between us. Try to be open to him," I said.

She closed her eyes, stayed quiet, and received him and his efforts to comfort her. That felt strange and comforting to me. She knew from a couple years before that I felt and heard Spirits, but we never spoke about it again.

As our drive continued, waves of emotions continued to rise and fall as my brain began comprehending that my brother was, in fact, gone; that I was here connecting with him, and I was about to go and see his dead body and meet his girlfriend for the first time.

There were many moments of silence just waiting to get to the town about twenty minutes south of our cottage where emergency helpers drove him.

We pulled into the parking lot and began the walk up to the small quaint hospital surrounded by forest trees, with the sun going down and dusk-like calm all around us.

I watched my father in and out of emotion as we all walked towards the doorway. We hugged and confirmed that we were all comfortable with what was about to occur. We agreed that seeing Ryan must be done, and that in some weird way, it would be comforting to see him one last time. It was like my brain needed to know for sure so it could register truly that this had indeed happened.

My father is one strong man in more ways that I can count or share in this book. He was the first to go in independently to see Ryan. My mother and I walked down the hall into the waiting room where Monica was waiting with her friends.

I knew about her; my brother shared a little, but not much. It was the strangest feeling we all shared later. It felt like we already knew her, there was a natural acceptance in our approach to comforting her.

We listened to her story of what happened, her tears, and how devastated and shocked she was. With heartache about how she felt and how we felt, we continued to hold space together. There was warmth being in the room with her, meeting her, and being together felt surprisingly good. Perhaps because we saw the happiness, positive changes, and Spirit-lifting possibilities that became present in Ryan's life with her in it. We finally got to see this special woman.

My dad returned from his visit to Ryan and came into the room. When he saw Monica for the first time, his eyes widened with a soft glow of happiness. His energy said, *There she is…it's her.* A broken heart replaced his expression and a wave of reality that now meant an end to his son's future with her.

It was our turn. I decided to be next, to go and see my brother alone.

As I walked through the doors, I watched the nurse's facial expressions and felt their discomfort and sadness as they watched me. I walked in with courage.

The police warned me it was a bit messy and that I didn't have to go in if I didn't want to. But, of course, I had to; it was all part of the process. The door opened, and there he was, under a white sheet.

A body is just a body after death takes place. Yet it was a body that I had known to be my brother for thirty years. I cried and held my heart with strength. I kept trying to remember when I hugged him last, when I heard his voice last.

I looked over his face and saw where he hit and skidded down. I noticed he was topless in his swim shorts with a broken collar bone sticking out of his shoulder. It was a bit painful to think of how this might have happened to him, and then I remembered his unique feet.

I felt emotional as memories of being kids briefly ran through my mind. I saw moments in my mind's eye we shared together and the small details of his expressions and body.

I lifted the white sheet and looked at his feet and touched them. He was cold, and I could feel the life force gone; what a strange feeling.

I walked around the room, talking out loud to him as if he could hear me. Weirdly, it felt like in just a moment he would wake up; his body still looked so life-like and natural, but his Spirit was gone. My mind was playing tricks on me, I suppose.

I realized that the day before, he was at my Nanny's house picking up sheets for bedding to take up to the cottage. At the time, I was sleeping there with my three-year-old. I heard his voice come in, and I wanted to wake up and see him and hug him, but my body said otherwise. When my Nanny went into the room where I was sleeping, she told me she was getting him sheets. Unaware that this was my last chance to get one last embrace, I felt a huge pull to wake up and hug him, but I didn't. I was a tired mother who was taking a good long rest.

So here now, back at the hospital seeing his body, I wept while taking my last hug. It was not the same; his hugs were warm, heart-felt, and honest. The gentle energy he provided when you swooped in to hug him was healing and comforting. So, I finished my prayer, looked at the wounds, and then left the room.

I watched my mother and Monica, arm in arm, take their turn, and I went outside to the edge of the trees and wept. I felt closer to God and the magic of the elements than ever before.

I spoke out loud for help to release the pain and help me accept. I requested to Ryan, and God: "Let me see him one last time."

Just like that, I could hear him, but this time instead of seeing him, his presence felt like he was part of the trees, and his energy surrounded me. *I am right here, Ashley,* I heard in my head, as the trees were shadowed, and the light from the sun had faded almost completely. I felt small because the trees were tall and offered me a supportive presence that surrounded the hospital and comforted me.

I turned and saw my dad walking over to me from the hospital's front doors and walked back to let him know I was okay. He informed me that we needed to drive to the cottage before it was too dark to pick up his truck, which was half an hour further North on Highway 35. I wanted to go with him and be at the cottage, by the lake where Ryan's death took place. Scared and committed, we checked on the other two and left together.

The drive was expressive, and with each of us having our memories and internal process, I was happy I was with my dad. To be his only daughter left behind has been a unique journey.

Thirty-minutes later we saw the familiar sign, to the gravel driveway to our cottage, aptly named Friendship Lane and felt a bitter sweetness that was anything but familiar.

Each weekend our family packed the car, loaded it, drove two hours, and spent the weekend traveling the forest like free birds, playing with neighbour kids at the cottages up the road, and having a blast in the sacred waters of Raven Lake. The lake doesn't have any limestone; it's surrounded by granite rock, so it's soft to touch and very clean. I sing to it almost every time I go.

We pulled onto the property and saw Ryan's small silver Ford truck parked there. My dad went to gather Ryan's belongings from the cottage and turned everything off, while I went to his vehicle. His shirt was inside; it smelled like him, too. You bet I took a huge whiff!

I saw the canoe parked on the dock; I looked at the sky I've looked at hundreds of times before as a child. The sky was deep blue black and twinkling stars filled the dark space, so many I could never count them all. It created a feeling of awe while I also felt like there was a hole in the middle of my chest. All I knew to do with the pain was cry and sing.

I sang *Amazing Grace* out loud, which always reminded me of our grandma Mable, on my dad's side. I made my own rendition of the song to express what I was feeling and surrendered to my grief.

2: Ryan's Story

July 11, 1987

The time had come. Ryan had been cooking in the oven for nine months, and his arrival was close. My mom rested on a chair in the shade on our century home porch situated in a quiet neighborhood. There were lots of mature trees that lined the streets; the old porch was covered and large enough that I was able to play close by while she rested, trying to receive a full breath. I was about four years old and a busy non-stop girl.

My Mom's belly was huge, as she's a petite woman and Ryan was brewing to be a big boy.

The summer heat without air conditioning made for an uncomfortable end to pregnancy. My mom didn't have her mother with her, as Agnes moved to Nova Scotia with Vince, my papa, just before Ryan was born. The loss of her mom's support was a great challenge at that time; she had and still does have an incredible faith within that carries her through many challenges.

The inside of my mom's pelvis was shaped like a funnel, and for a healthy natural birth, it needed to be a tunnel. She was in hard labor for ten hours as Ryan was too large and became stressed and stuck. My dad yelled and demanded the doctor to make a move, leading to an emergency C-section. If you ever needed someone to have your back and get things sorted out, he was your man.

After I had been delivered, I had a long indent in my forehead for a week from the narrow emergence. Ryan's big melon head was a different story. We used to joke that because it was a good large head, when he and I collided I'd be left crying and he laughed at me, as it didn't hurt him one bit.

Upon beginning the C-section, the doctor discovered that Ryan was floating in meconium, which is very dangerous to a baby's health. I share this because many studies now show that the experience in the womb, during and after delivery, impacts a baby's psychological development. Anxiety can arise from many different factors pre- and post-birth.

Ryan's struggles didn't end there. He had, what doctors believed at the time, colic. He screamed, cried, and would almost turn blue from pain and upset for nine months straight. Our family home consisted of me, four years old, my youngest half-brother Peter, thirteen years old, and my parents. My dad got a second job to add to his full-time one to get out of the house, as he couldn't hold a screaming baby or tolerate listening for long, either. My mom was isolated and exhausted but continued to rock, soothe, and keep Ryan close through these months.

Let me tell you, the power and love of a mother; she's a star.

Ryan would get four-hour breaks out of sheer exhaustion where he would fall asleep on my mother. My dad's brother Pete came when he could to listen to my mom vent, and only one other woman was able to come to take a turn holding Ryan occasionally, to give her relief. She was a lady named Leona, a friend of my brother Peter's mother.

Later in Ryan's first year, they determined that he had a hernia, which explained so much of his pain.

Ryan's start to life was strained, thwarted, and disconnected from his dad. His pain was burdensome and his opportunity to explore the world was hindered.

As he healed and grew up from baby stage, he bloomed into life with passion, joy, hilarity, zest, and spirit. Ryan was a happy boy, so much fun to be with, the class clown and fearless one. It's fair to say that he got off to a rocky start in life, which impacted his development. Worthy of note was the powerful spirit that brightened and guided him through his struggles. You could see and feel his brightness if you knew him.

In the years that followed, he played hours of Lego and outdoor games with neighbor friends and me. In our backyard we had a huge old maple tree that would turn into our time machine. We had a deep backyard for endless hours of playing. We spent countless hours in the woods at our family cottage playing creatively, coming home when we heard my mom's wicked loud whistle telling us it was lunch or dinnertime.

Ryan was an empathetic boy whose heart would get hurt deeply. He struggled to feel included with friends and would take social challenges to heart. Ryan would run or hide when he was hurt; he was very private that way. He felt for others beyond the norm, as his empathic abilities were solid and real. There wasn't an awareness of being highly empathic at the time; the belief at that time was toughen up, get in there and be a big boy.

I remember he would sit in my room at such a young age and listen to me so compassionately. I was lucky to have him there with me. He would follow all my crazy ideas and give so openly with his heart. As a big sister, I took advantage of that from time to time.

Ryan went to French immersion school. He was kind and hilarious, and his peers loved him, yet being so sensitive and empathic, he would get taken advantage of by some friends and the odd bully. At times he would instigate situations; it was his wit and zest, but sometimes it found him trouble. Ryan had deep compassion for many people, perhaps because he felt deeply himself and was raised in a family that valued respect for self and others.

My dad was always in our corners, preparing us with his street smarts, as he was on them at a very young age. "Be ready to defend yourself at any time; I will have your back," he would say.

I think that was about the time he put us both into karate. If we had trouble with school or a teacher, watch out; you wouldn't want to mess with our dad.

Ryan was very particular about how tight his hockey gear needed to be, how certain clothes didn't feel right, socks needed to be high and tight on his legs. I often remember waking up to full meltdowns with hockey gear not tight enough and my dad's loud attempts to get things moving or slamming of doors leaving him behind. He used to take off his hockey equipment and have red marks where the tight tape had been.

Ryan offered family members the warmest hugs, and all the Acadian nannies and aunties just adored him, giving him so much affirmation and attention when we would visit. Almost every summer we visited Nova Scotia; that's where our grandparents were born, raised, and lived. Family was important to Ryan, and so were his friends.

When Ryan experienced hurt, a lot of the time, he would hold it in or only share very little. Unfortunately, it became too tricky academically for him halfway through French immersion elementary school and he needed to move schools.

This school change was another challenging part of his life experience that hurt my parents. My parents believed it was important to share because they think it was a critical factor in Ryan's later years of active addiction, and something we all could be a whole lot more open about and stand to support.

Being a sensitive empathic person is like being highly attuned to the feelings and emotions of others. The ability to discern what's being felt goes beyond empathy; Ryan took on feelings of others on a deep emotional, sometimes physical level, and stayed quiet about it. After moving schools Ryan experienced extreme bullying from peers in grade seven, and his teacher failed to support him. I believe it's hard to transfer schools when puberty begins, and groups of friends are already established. No good reason to excuse the behaviors though.

At that time, the board of education was beginning to mandate and enforce bullying awareness and procedures to follow. Before that, many things went unnoticed, un-dealt with, or even ignored. Once Ryan started at the new school, he would get chased in the schoolyard at recesses, while some days kids threw oranges at him as he ran away. The portable was unsupervised at lunch, so bullies continued to pick on kids without notice. One short young boy was forced into the garbage can many times. Ryan finally had enough of watching it. He stood up to protect the boy, challenged the bullies, and fought them, removing the kid from the garbage one day. Despite his efforts, Ryan then turned into the next target, and it continued to escalate from there. After my dad found Ryan's sweater with orange stains on it and Ryan finally confessed his troubles, my father was angry and called a meeting with the teacher.

Ryan cried and spilled his heart out, letting her know what was happening every day. Unfortunately, she did nothing about it, and the empty support impacted his trust and ability to open again. For Ryan, this ruptured him profoundly, and he was never the same after. My parents fought with the teacher, the principal, and the board office; they got nowhere, and the bullying continued.

Later my father found out that the secretary at the school board had connections with the principal who was about to retire; little changes were going to be made. My parents finally decided to switch schools but had concerns that one of the kids' bullying was going to move with Ryan. Answered prayers, perhaps; that boy ended up stabbing someone and was no longer able to attend any school. I know bullying still happens, and there has been a shift in support, awareness, and help that has changed in schools. Thankfully.

Ryan went to counselors at a young age but struggled to trust them and chose not to open. He wasn't ready to be vulnerable again. Later in active addiction, he found some safe space with a couple of counselors, but the follow-through proved to be a significant challenge and never really took.

Ryan moved to the new school with little trouble and finished grade eight. While out in the schoolyard, Ryan noticed another kid getting bullied in the yard. He went right up to the kid and told him, "I got your back."

The kid didn't believe him and said, "Yeah right."

Ryan didn't give up; he said, "I know what it's like, and I mean it; I got your back."

He continued to watch out for that boy while finishing school.

He saw himself in another and chose to stand for them, and that is just a beautiful example of empathy and compassion this world needs more of. Even just one person standing up can create a difference for another.

It was when Ryan left middle school that he began self-medicating. It was subtle at first and unfortunately grew in usage and choice over ten years.

In high school Ryan was a thick, solid rugby player; the principal and coach told my dad that Ryan had "balls of steel." He got along okay academically and with friends, but the inner conflicts continued to stay tucked away, and the addiction became more apparent. He searched for a means of coping and tried hard to find thrill and joy.

Once high school was over, the addiction got worse. Ten years on and off, it was a lot to support as a family. Many days our family was concerned if he would even make it home alive.

I'm sure some of you may resonate with active addiction being unpredictable; it's scary, it can be heartbreaking, sad, and exhausting watching someone you love slowly to slip away from what you knew them to be. Through it all as a family, we learned to stick together and be there for each other, while also setting boundaries.

It meant a lot to our family how many times Ryan would stand for others in the face of his hurt. It was like his soul's path was to come here, feel the depth of pain, and heal by being the example himself. He's a hero in my eyes and has changed my life in many ways.

I saw Ryan suffer silently for so many years, and even with attempts to get him help, he continued to hold back or would watch multiple movies together with my dad to distract himself from life. Watching an orchestrated reality play out on the screen probably took him away from his own pains. As he entered his twenties, Ryan would grind at work and use my dad as a soundboard late at night to talk his stress out. My dad showed up huge for Ryan in ways that no one will really know; I will always remember that. Ryan would find other people to help wherever he went; even when he was sick, he still took a bunch of his friends to the cottage to make sure they had a good time while he slept and woke up to stoke the fire and eat.

When we lose people, their stories become comforting tales that keep their Spirits alive through our words, laughter, and admiration. Ryan was very loved, and these short stories from my dad illustrate his character and heart.

Ryan would go up to our cottage in Dorset, Ontario with my dad as a young man. They got settled in, unpacked, and cooked some dinner together. Ryan soon left to drive and meet a friend. He drove twenty minutes away to meet a girl he knew.

In their short time together, she was stuck and needed to get home two hours away.

Without question, Ryan drove her all the way home; now, at the time, there were no cell phones in our family, so my dad got worried and went to the lake landing to use a Bell payphone to call home to my mother. She confirmed that Ryan was indeed there and had made the long trip to help a friend. Fuming mad, my dad stayed up and counted his blessings that he was okay.

After high school, Ryan had many buddies within his hometown, and one night, his friend Brad was in trouble. To this day, it seemed like Ryan was in the right place at the right time; I also question if he had an intuitive pull to be there. Brad had ten guys chasing him out of a bar down the road. Ryan was nearby in his car and witnessed the chase. He came flying down the road and swerved to a halt, cutting off all the guys from reaching his friend. His help gave Brad enough time to jump into hiding in a nearby bush. Ryan drove off quickly after finding a parking spot and then ran in Brad's direction. He quietly called out to Brad when he heard his voice from the bush. Ryan stayed in the bush with his friend for two hours until they felt safe to go back to his car. It sounds crazy, but his buddies shared this story in the garage after his funeral and boy, did we ever laugh.

Ryan worked for four years at a mushroom farm before getting hired by the Catholic school board as a custodian. He struggled at this workplace with mental health, navigating social interactions and coping with negativity from his supervisor. He adored the workers; some were kind ladies, as he would put it, and some men from Guatemala with whom he played soccer.

Now there was a particular chemical used to clean the mushrooms, and many of the ladies were not using proper protective gear when spraying. Ryan looked further into the substances and realized it was dangerous for them, which the ladies didn't know about themselves. So, he stood up to the supervisor and demanded he investigate the safety procedures needed. The supervisor got very angry with Ryan as he needed to put further safety gear in place, but Ryan won the affection of the women he helped. They were so grateful for his caring heart.

Ryan was at the school board as a custodian before he died. He loved this job because he could do his work independently, be helpful to teachers and students, and go at his own pace.

One day, custodians were sitting inside the break room and noticed a UPS delivery truck arriving at the school. It was pouring rain, and the school had construction piles outside. The man got his truck stuck in the deep mud. While the workers watched the man struggle, Ryan decided to go out in the pouring rain to help him. Ryan tried to push him out with no luck. Then he found some wood in the scrap pile near the construction site to place under the wheels so he could drive out.

The driver and Ryan were soaked to the bone, but they did it. The UPS driver thanked him and said he was such a kind person.

When he returned inside, some fellow workers put him down by calling him names for getting out there, thinking he was showing off. The supervisor later found Ryan and told him that was one hell of a kind act.

It seemed that Ryan was met with challenges or mean encounters wherever he went, yet he continued to stay humanly compassionate as he navigated relationships with others and his internal struggles. I often wonder if Ryan's life would have been different if he could have accepted the support he needed at that young age.

3: Ashley's Story

October 26, 1983

I was my mom's first child, and throughout my time in the oven, she was very energetic. She rode her bike to work at eight months pregnant and had crazy amounts of energy while I was in there. Guess I came by that honestly.

From a young age, as far as I can remember, I had an abundance of energy that shook through my whole body. I was alive as could be with so much inner- 'chi'—which is 'universal energy'—I didn't always know what to do with it all.

My mom was in labor with me for twenty-seven hours and my dad acted like he worked there. My mom is sure he was in the way a couple times because he was so eager to help and be part of the action. As mentioned before, my mom's pelvis was a tight squeeze, so at twenty-seven hours, they needed to pull me out with tools. I had a long dent in my forehead from trying to get out of her funnel-shaped pelvis, which soon disappeared.

When I came out, my parents described me as a perfect little specimen. My ears, nose, and mouth were so tiny and cute. When my dad's mother Mabel arrived, she said, "Good thing Ashley took after our side for her facial features, the French side have larger ones." They laughed.

As an infant, it was encouraged on my mom's side at that time not to hold me too much. Generational beliefs surely shift decisions we make, consciously or unconsciously. My mom and I began with a rupture in our intimate connection early on, but we've intended together all these later years to heal and come together even closer and stronger. For that, I'm grateful.

As a baby I was healthy, easy-going, amusing and content. I was able to pike my body and use my leg to get out of the crib at a young age. As a two-year-old I would stand my ground telling my mom often, "ASHIE DO IT!" demanding I do things myself. I was busy, curious, and independent. I was outside often and surrounded by lots of loving family as a young one.

When it came to drop-off at school, I'd run to find my dad hiding in the coat rack, as I was not impressed to be left there and attending school was not very enjoyable as I remember it.

You would find me doing cartwheels in houses, running off to neighbors without telling anyone and then wondering why people were mad. I stole icing tubes and hid under the bed eating them all trying not to get caught, until my mom came to clean under the bed and found my empties. I guess I wasn't conscious enough to clean up the empty containers.

I absolutely hated anything tight on my skin, which meant that ballet and dance class had many tears and tantrums, where I refused to wear tights or any dresses. My mom babysat two of my best friends after school and we attended dance together. They reminded me that I ended up stealing the teacher's whistle and fooling around in most classes. That didn't last long. I became alive in gymnastics, horseback riding, and baseball.

Throughout my early years I was a bit of a wild animal. This would lead to some friends at school asking what was wrong with me. It resulted in most of my report cards saying, "If Ashley would just stop talking, she would be able to focus and do so much better." Sitting in a chair at school was torture sometimes; I could feel all the sensations from my pants on my body, and the way my shirt bunched up. I'd get caught up with what other people were thinking or doing. Other times I would just imagine other places and things to escape school.

I stayed quiet and contained in class because I feared judgment and embarrassment, resulting in only having a couple close friends and being teased and bullied by other kids throughout my school years. I also had my hands in kicking boys in the butt with pointy shoes and once joining the boys in bullying another kid, which to this day I am not impressed with myself about. Totally not cool.

In grade four I remember the teacher would randomly call on kids to answer questions from the board. I was so anxious she would call on me that while sitting, I would be in a state of freeze praying she wouldn't say my name or ask me to answer anything.

All these irritations and sensitivities kept me from listening to a lot of what teachers were saying, and most of my academic years I needed one on one tutors to get through. English, art, and gym were my things!

I really didn't like school, until I went to college and got to pick what I wanted to learn. Even in college, I struggled to sit still; my fingers were pushing the pen on and off, or I was chewing on pen lids or falling asleep in the class with a monotone teacher. I did well academically and in my work placements because my heart was in it. My parents agreed to pay half of my tuition, and I had to get a job and pay the other half, so that I learned to put my own effort and money into what I wanted. I value that lesson a lot today.

At night from very young is when I'd have anxious thoughts, deep questions about the world. "Where do I go when I die? Is it all black and no one is there?" I had wondering emotions and thoughts of all kinds from the day-to-day occurrences. I didn't realize I needed help with all the energies I was picking up on or guidance to help me navigate. I didn't realize I could try to talk about them; everyone was busy, we were sent to bed with a kiss and a hug. At night my mind was the loudest. I stayed isolated, anxious, and alone for many years.

As I grew older, I would poke and bug people, adults especially, because I could see and feel things even they didn't know sometimes. I got a kick out of making people uncomfortable. I got so used to living with being uncomfortable that, at the time, it made my younger self feel better to give it to someone else. I learned the hard way many times that my lack of impulse control was hurtful, and I learned to think first before I spoke. That took maturity and many years of practice.

When I was in my own space with close friends and family, the wild, fun Ashley came out. This is where Ryan comes in. He was also full of zest and energy, which I shared above. Although he had a rough go at birth and through school, he and I were best friends when we were young. We were four years apart, which was great in the younger years, but we drifted a bit as I moved on from high school.

As young kids we would play for hours in the woods together making forts out of branches, pines, and anything we could find lying around the cottage. We joined friends outdoors with our bikes, played manhunt or games at the park. We created Lego villages, we had wild imagination games, skipping, water blaster guns, sprinklers, and silly pranks on each other or others that made us laugh so hard. It was those moments that brought us the closest. We played sports together and loved our many family gatherings that were filled with music, games, food, and laughter.

On Christmas Eve and Easter nights we would have a sleepover in my old wooden framed double bed because we were so excited. I loved being his sister and he was an incredible brother. He would always listen, as I never stopped talking, but he would listen with his whole heart, and I could feel how much he loved me.

I used to bug him and not always be fair to him. I would ask him to tickle my back before bed and tell him I would tickle his back after. Then I would pretend to be sleeping, but I wasn't, and he would be so sad and hurt. Sometimes I would hug him so hard that he would cry and then I would say sorry. Sibling digs and older sister power trips. As we grew up, I made right with him. I apologized, letting him know he deserved so much better. I promised never to mistreat him or take advantage of his kindness again. I affirmed to him that I had his back.

When it came to bullies, when I could be there, you bet I was. One day my dad asked me to follow Ryan to the park. He was twelve at the time and had shifted schools, and he was going to challenge a kid who was bullying him. I didn't think twice and threw on my shoes and followed him down the block. Where my dad came from, if you were being pushed around or bullied, the best thing to do was push back and show your strength.

Ryan challenged the young boy to a fight at the park where a couple other kids stood watching. There was a tall pine tree, a slab of cement, and one old metal basketball net. I stood beside the grass and there on the cement the boys swung, grabbed, and pushed each other. I stood right beside him, hands crossed at my front, giving him the confidence he needed to stand up and show that he wouldn't be pushed around anymore.

The young boy left the park after Ryan's last swing connected with his face and from that day forward, they were friends. Ryan joined him and a couple of other boys from then on. Our family still connects with them to this day.

When Ryan was fifteen years old three other boys jumped him walking home from a dishwashing job at a pub in town. The walk was five blocks home, and he took the neighborhood route. I had just picked up a friend who arrived from Nova Scotia, and my husband, who at the time was my boyfriend. We were hanging out at our family home.

Ryan arrived at the door with blood on his face and said, "Three guys just jumped me!" I had shoes on and was out that door faster than you can imagine and ran down the road after them like an antelope.

The other two threw on shoes and weren't far behind me. The three thugs had run a block ahead, but I was able to catch up with my killer tippy toe running. I still use it to this day and kids always say, "How do you run so fast?" Now you know one of my secrets. I was close enough to see where the boys were running. I ran past a main road, down an ice hill not slipping, through an alley beside a building and around a street toward the house they were running into. I got a hold of one boy and held his arm behind his back while Brandon and my friend caught up and helped me. We ended up calling the police and later Ryan had to go identify one of the boys. No one messed with my family!

Along with the wild side as a young person I had many emotional meltdowns, and so did Ryan. His consisted of sensory meltdowns as explained before. My tantrums were due to unregulated emotions, tight clothing, or not getting my way. I'd bang or hit doors so hard it sounded like they were coming off the hinges. I had unpredictable mood swings that came out of nowhere, crying and rude remarks. My mom stopped allowing me to go on sleepovers with friends because I would chug cans of pop and ate Cheezies and goodies, to then return home one heck of a monster with little to no sleep. A little much for everyone!

Often, I was happy to venture out into nature by myself. When I was in nature I never felt alone. It always felt like a safe place, where I imagined things I wanted, I had freedom to roam without judgment, and energy was calm, so my emotions were easier to navigate. My grand father Vince had a vision to build a cottage. He took my grand mother Agnes whom I mentioned in the first chapter with her sister and husband and made it a reality.

A family cottage that hosted so many friends and family over the last forty years that became a regulating space to explore, heal, and come together. It also had its challenges with ownership and money responsibilities amongst family members that had its moments.

I am forever grateful to have grown up there. My papa was born and raised on the East coast of Cape Breton Island. The heritage and Spirit of the Acadians is truly something special. They are such a proud community and celebrate their ancestors and history each year through stories, dance, crafts, events, and historical locations.

It became a part of us and is a large component of my deep connection to nature and family. Growing up outdoors, my papa often escaped to the woods, fished, hunted, and lost himself amongst the trees. I've always been able to relate to that; nature has a way of co-regulating with me. The small intricate things happening in nature inspire me. Nature gives so much without taking much back at all. Growing up sensitive has taught me that I need to rest to process, take breaks and tune into myself often instead of pushing past my boundaries and waiting for a crash to catch my breath.

Over the years I shared warmth, tears, fun, laughter, songs, and so much more. I feel blessed by the colorful experiences. I've had a depth since I was young that many people expressed as being "an old soul" or "wiser than her years." I just think I'm in tune with something deep in my heart.

Back then I wasn't aware, and my family didn't know either, that I was able to feel the energy of others and struggled to regulate my own. I relate this to being an Empath.

In my own words, an Empath is someone who can feel and sense within their own body and energy field the feelings, intentions, or thoughts of others as their own. It can be a beautiful gift when in the helping profession, as a healer, being a compassionate friend, or an understanding parent. I can sense emotions or thoughts before they are actualized by others or said out loud. It's also challenging to know what's mine and what's someone else's' or where to draw the line of what to share or how to respectfully listen.

Where was I to put that energy after I received it? How was I supposed to unpack that much feeling with such a wild Spirit already so young?

Often, I didn't unpack it; now I understand that I just sucked it in or tucked it away inside. When I got older, I used friendships to talk things out, but my friends were also young and didn't understand either. Due to that confusion on both our parts, I began to feel shame and guilt about it all. I began believing there was something wrong with me, so I tried my best to please and fit in.

As a young child the array of emotions were already enough, let alone other people's too. I knew when my parents were fighting even if it was quiet. I knew when there was an unhealthy discord between my parents and their family members without the details. I knew when people were talking behind my back. I knew when waves of emotion were going to increase before they happened.

I felt things so deeply and on such a large scale I didn't always know what was happening or feel safe within myself. I became hyper fixated on other people's feelings so I could be ready, on guard or flee to feel safe. Over the years of not detecting anxiety and ADHD characteristics, I developed co-dependent behaviors. This in my own words is when I rely on helping or fixing people, places, and things to feel worthy of being here or safe. I learned to push past my own needs to be there for others because when other people were good, I could feel good too, in an Empathic way. With years of these behaviors, I am recovering and developing new pathways of choice, health, and feeling worthy, safe, and able to stay in my lane.

Growing up, my father stood beside my mom and was a huge financial support for her to complete eleven years of university part-time from home while raising us. She got into teacher's college and became a teacher; I'm so proud of her hard work and my father's dedication to our family. Many of those studying years left me with limited mom time unless I was sick. My brother and I often roamed the cottage and visited friends with my dad. He kept us busy and away so my mom could study. It was just the way it was.

I wanted to be close to my mom but instead I got mad at her and acted out towards her without knowing the underlying feelings or how to articulate them. It felt hard, troubled, sharp, annoying, and disconnected between us for such a long time. I got in trouble with her a lot because of it, which in turn continued the shame and feeling wrong cycle.

My dad was like my friend and at times, my parents would fight over us kids. I'd like to normalize that; there are so many decisions that parents need to make for their children. The unhealed parts were brought into the family that also set us up to heal them together.

My dad was very young when he had two boys, Paul and Peter, who are my half-brothers. When he joined the loving family foundation from my mom's family, it offered us all a lot of heart.

Parenting comes with so many challenges. I am present myself as a parent to the way we come face to face with ourselves while parenting our children. Sometimes we are not ready to go there, and it can take years to be ready and willing. That's okay, we can heal together.

The light side is that both my parents gave Ryan and I many extra opportunities to grow and enjoy and I know they did their best with what they were given. They supported my half-brothers in many ways too. It can take a whole lifetime to unpack the experiences we grow up with from our families or caregivers. That's part of human life and self-realization, and I'm thankful to be at their side today still learning together.

My parents have incredible hearts; they are hardworking family people and along this grief path we have grown so much together.

When I became a teenager—now those were confusing times! I'm sure many people can relate. Developmentally, I tried to figure out who I was, why I struggled with things and questioned my purpose. I often withheld my feelings or needs out of fear that I would be criticized, judged, or not heard. I hid anxiety and low self-esteem that I felt and pushed myself to be brave, to fit in and have fun. At times this took its toll on me, while other times I was silly, playful, and tried hard to pass my classes.

I was confused by navigating all the different people I encountered. I often helped others but felt guilty in taking up space with my own needs. I didn't understand at the time that I was empathic and sensitive. It's apparent to me now that I am a Highly Sensitive Person, also known as an HSP. I found this researched term over the last five years from Dr. Elaine Aron; check her out if you're curious.

In my own words and experience, a highly sensitive person is someone who has a very sensitive nervous system and is deeply impacted by social, emotional, and physical stimuli. So, being in large crowds—although I'm an extrovert—can drain me, and I can feel exhausted after a short while. Since I grew up pushing past my limits to please others, I would over-give, share, and shine my energy out to feel safe or good about myself. Over time, this led me to four different burnouts before the age of forty.

The moods of certain people can feel toxic to me, leaving me feeling ill or signaling to my body to hide or get away. I have had allergic reactions to most common antibiotics and perfumes and what I eat changes the way my brain functions. Again, all this I learned in my thirties through self-discovery, natural professionals, and elimination diets as I got candida in my system under control. I used to have symptoms of overgrowth in yeast as a young kid and just suffered in my room, never telling anyone and feeling bad about what more was wrong with me. I learned later the gut had a huge part in my moods and emotional overwhelm and meltdowns.

If I eat dairy and refined sugars, I experience brain fog; words can be hard to locate, I can get moody, anxious, irritable and experience inflammation and pain in my joints. When I avoid them, I am clearer in my focus; thinking and organizing takes less effort. With my exceptionalities, focus and regulating still takes a lot of effort and skill. Sleep and exercise are imperative along with healthy choices in food.

Watching horror or violence on TV or in person is just plain no! It's painful and uncomfortable in my body. It feels like I'm in the event, not just watching it. Another reason why video games are unappealing to me: my whole-body tenses and I get overwhelmed. But simple ones I can enjoy for a short while.

Change and transitions can also be challenging as an HSP. Let's say I never really liked them, but over time I've learned tools and strategies to help me navigate them. Change and transitions used to look like over-thinking to the point where I couldn't sleep or settle.

Playing over and over things I would say if they happened, or if someone said this, I would say that. Second-guessing everything I thought and calling three to six people for advice or ideas before deciding on something. I stopped listening to my body and lived outside of it the best I could. Until injuries, mental health, and wellness became apparent that something had to change, or I was going down a bad road.

As shared, I went to college and studied to be a Child & Youth Counselor where I learned a lot about myself. Helping children and youth at risk became a huge part of my life, discovering exceptionalities, solutions and community of helpers out there.

My first burn out was in Australia where I studied my BA in Youth Work. I worked at a group home for youth and many of them were on the streets unless they decided to come home. Another youth was placed there because she had nowhere else to live and this was not the best place for her needs. It was inconsistent, staffing was hit or miss, and I did overnights while studying during the day. This offered me some spending money on trips and adventures, and I could work on the weekends while studying during the week.

One evening while on an overnight shift, I had one client who was a minor prostitution sex worker. She returned home quickly, said hi, and locked herself in her room. The sun went down, I continued to clean up and tried to approach her, when suddenly her pimp tried to break into the house. I went into fight mode; she called me into her room and locked the door behind me. She appeared to be on an assortment of drugs, while reaching into a fanny pack to get Valium to calm herself down. She let me know who it was but didn't admit why he was there. My guess was that she took the fanny of drugs, but I continued to stay calm for her.

All she kept saying was, "I wish my mom was here, she would kill him." He continued banging on the door and windows, but finally subsided. I stayed at her doorway until she fell asleep and then went to the room beside her, wrote my incident report, and took another hour to fall asleep myself.

After that day and report writing, I found out this wasn't the first time, and in the past no workers in the home wanted to go to the police out of fear. I just couldn't deny what happened, so I went to the police station, and they took my statement about the man and event.

In my heart I felt like I was doing the right thing, but then it got worse. Without the pimp, she was not protected, and I witnessed older men coming to the house for her. It was too much for me to handle. I sought help from my supervisor, but their hands were tied, unless I wanted to talk to her about safe brothels that were available. Due to my sensitive nature, I stopped taking shifts and took a break to recover emotionally and mentally.

A month later I returned to my supervisor to give my notice and returned for one more shift. I decided that I needed to face that space one last time. Like when you fall off a horse, you need to get right back on so you're not afraid the next time. I took a bus, walked half hour to get to the home, and talked to myself the whole time. I experienced good connections with both girls that were there.

The young girl I stood for asked me to walk her to the train station, as another staff member stayed with the second girl. We laughed and shared along the walk and to my surprise we met her pimp at the train station as he had just gotten out of jail. What a huge lesson in my life that was, to let go with love, trusting that I did as much as I could at the time. I cried most of the walk back home and finished that shift with dignity and respect for everyone, including myself. I learned my limits and chose another job at the university as a note writer for students in need; it paid well too.

I kept a picture of that one girl for a very long time to tune in with her energy and send her light prayers. I felt the shift when it no longer felt like she was alive, and the picture became an empty feeling. I prayed for her soul's peace.

My second burn out came from being in an ungrounded relationship far away from my friends and family. Although I met wonderful new friends, I was hired as a supervisor of a childcare program and loved living the outdoor opportunities of BC; the relationship was complex for us both. Our own inner conflicts banged up against each other in an unhealthy way.

Throughout my time there we did so many outdoor activities. While snowboarding on a mountain, I pushed a little too much on the last run, when my legs were already tired. Weeks later after a three-hour bike ride near the ocean I fully tore two parts of my knee, leaving me with an injury that took a year to get healed by surgery. Without my family, foundational support, and understanding my sensitivities, that burn out became a true gift, because it led me to another breaking point.

I realized I was not in the right place for me; the relationship was hurting me from the inside out. I learned lessons that helped me value my family and the relationship needs that would bring me health. My mother was so concerned for my wellbeing that she bought me a ticket and flew me from British Columbia to Nova Scotia, where I landed into care and my roots from childhood, and it brought me back to myself. I returned to BC and chose to leave everything to move home with my parents. I cleaned up my health, slowly integrated back into working, reunited with my husband, and then entered back into my profession and started a family.

I choose to share this with you so you can understand that it took me almost forty years to tame her, discover her, support her, and yet it will continue for all my life. I'm learning to harness the unlimited source energy that flows through my center. I'm thirty-nine years old and I've learned a lot about my past experiences, my nervous system, how my brain functions, what my exceptionalities are, and how to care for my mental, emotional, and spiritual needs.

In my Reiki practice, I channel energies to help people shift and let go. I listen with my gifts to discover together what's holding people back, what's possible, and small steps that can be explored to get there. I invest every day in staying grounded and healthy to continue being of service to young people, adults, and my family.

Mediumship has been a part of my experience for a very long time. It's something that I keep a distance from at different times considering all that I navigate day by day. Being a support for people, places, and things can feel like enough, let alone adding Spirits to the mix.

I never expected I would be using those skills to connect with my own brother after his death, and how that experience would change my life.

4: Gifts Through Grief

2016

I sang to the stars while sitting on a large protruding rock close to the water's edge.

Dad had collected all of Ryan's belongings from inside the cottage. I saw the glow of lights coming from the window go out. I took one last curious look at the large blue canoe that Ryan had taken out on the lake that morning with Monica.

We had to leave with both vehicles; it was very late at this point. I drove my brother's truck while my dad drove his car to meet our neighbor, Mom, and Monica back at the hospital. The exhaustion that followed shock, pain, and sadness started to sink in.

As I left the cottage, I felt like part of me wanted to stay behind. Leaving the cottage always came with a heavy heart, as a kid, but especially these days.

I drove up the steep rocky hill to the highway and followed my dad. It was dark and it made me feel so much more tired. Many things ran through my mind; waves of emotions continued.

We got about halfway back to the hospital when my brother's Spirit dropped into the truck's passenger seat. He appeared full body, with jeans and a t-shirt, but had a translucent tone. His energy felt like he was alive. He felt fresh, excited, accessible, and happy!

He said, *Hi Ashley!* I was taken back by his voice because feeling and hearing a dead brother created a ripple effect of shock as I tried to reality-check myself. My mind felt like it was receiving brain shocks. *Is this really happening?*

I instantly cried and told him I loved him and couldn't believe this had happened.

He continued to ride in the truck with me for about ten long minutes.

While I drove, he said, *I feel great! I feel so free!* His tone of voice that I heard in my head took a lot to process. When I felt and saw him earlier, his experience was shock, anger, and disappointment. I pieced together that it had been about two or three hours after he came through on the car ride to the hospital.

"Now you feel free?" I questioned.

What I experienced in my body at that point was a rush of excitement and energy. *What happened to him in those couple of hours?* I wondered.

It's not my story to tell. I sensed that an incredible story existed in his transition to the other side, but he did not share enough details with me about that transition for me to write about it here.

As I spoke with him, he shared a message he wanted me to give Monica. I agreed and then felt his incredible love and strength; he said, *I have to go back to her!*

I then witnessed his Spirit body turn into what looked like little hologram squares breaking apart into so many pieces, and with a gust of wind, he flew out the front of the truck, into the sky, and off in the direction of the hospital.

When I arrived at the hospital about fifteen minutes later, I felt a little uneasy and nervous about sharing the message. It was not new to my family that I saw and communicated with Spirits, but we were all vulnerable.

I had a close bond with my brother that only a couple of people in my life genuinely understood. I trusted his Spirit, and that gave me the courage to trust what he asked me to share. So, I told the family of my experience with Ryan's truck and then told Monica his message: *When you are in the kitchen cooking, remember me. Feel my hands touching you, and you will feel me.* His message rang faithfully to her, and she appeared to find comfort in his words, even in her vulnerable state.

We parted ways, driving separately; I fell asleep in the vehicle my neighbor drove me home in. Words and talking just seemed too hard. We had let Monica know we would see her soon and wanted to be there for her; I promised my brother I would.

Getting in the doorway of my home, I felt comforting relief, yet I was still in a daze. I felt numb, sad, and didn't know what to do with myself. I took a sweater that belonged to Ryan from our parents' house before I left to return home. I curled up into my bed, held the sweater in my arms, and smelled his scent with all I had. The smell brought comfort and pain. I wished I could have kept that smell forever, but it disappeared in a couple of days like my brother had.

The days that followed were hard on our family. It was the first time I left my two boys with their dad to care for their needs for a week. Most days I returned later in the day or sometimes after bedtime. I left each morning to be at my parents' house; upon waking the first morning, I felt a peaceful buzz through my body that lasted a couple of seconds until I woke further and realized that he had died. I felt like I was waking into a nightmare.

Driving his truck provided me with some comfort and familiar scents that I counted on each day. Day two, I arrived in town at my friend Linda's to process. I pulled into her driveway and there he was in the truck again. Ryan appeared bright, passionate, excited, and ready for action.

He said, *Let's get to work, my partner in crime.* I was still getting used to him arriving unexpectedly; I was also processing sadness in contrast to his excitement. I cried and smiled, thinking, *what is he talking about?*

Ryan didn't stay long that time, as I felt overwhelmed with emotion trying to make sense of my experiences and process my feelings of grief. So, I closed my energy off and ignored him; he disappeared, and I went into my friend's house to talk with her.

The "partners in crime" made sense to me years later, as many intuitive messages do. For me, messages inspire thoughts, ideas, or feelings that lead me towards other things. Years later I realized his messages together with my ability to listen, articulate, and hold space with our family, was how we transformed and healed our family lineage.

The traumatic impact of shock stayed with our family for years to come, especially for my oldest son. He began school for the first-time days after my brother passed, while our younger son stayed home with my husband.

When it was time to bring him to school, I walked him down a long hallway and into the class. He was very nervous and unsure about being there. He only knew my home daycare and the care of family members. I was barely holding myself together, when the teacher asked who I was.

I said, "This is Jack and I'm Ashley."

Her facial expression was odd and concerned as she asked me if I was okay.

I looked at Jack, who had walked in towards the cubbies looking back at me with concern and anxiety in his eyes. I told her, "I just lost my brother a couple days ago." Then I waved goodbye to Jack, turned around, and left. I cried as I walked down the hallway. That still is an experience I'm forgiving myself for.

Writing this, I realized how unfair that must have felt for him in senior kindergarten. He is one highly sensitive and exceptional human, too. At that time, I couldn't be a present mom.

He got a grief counselor two years later; with homeschooling through 2020 I was able to hold him in tears when waves of grief began to surface, listen to his heart, and process and articulate the feelings he couldn't express after it first happened.

It helped us to revisit the root of rupture, which was when I wasn't there, and he couldn't articulate and cope with the emotions from loss and so much change. With family support and professional help, we healed over time with patience and love.

For my parents, the week after Ryan's death, we processed plenty with one another, looked at pictures, talked with visitors, cried, hugged, organized, and at times sat silently together.

My physical presence was needed with my parents, as much as I needed them.

Luckily, I have two older half-brothers, and being in their presence brought me deep healing, especially their hugs. Monica arrived at our home that week with a courageous heart.

To see her felt unreal, as we had only heard little bits about her. She had hidden treasures of Ryan that unfolded over the next month.

Family members and friends came in and out of the house, and the second day, Monica approached us with pictures of their last day together.

That final day began slowly; they drove into town, where they climbed the famous Tower in Dorset, Ontario. Monica took many individual pictures of Ryan, the majestic landscapes in the background, and their intimate embraces together.

If you knew Ryan, this was not his favorite thing to do. He would delete pictures of himself without you knowing, as he judged himself quite harshly. He wore either a full, happy smile or an uncertain smirk. These pictures showed us the most genuine, honest, and beautiful photos we had ever seen of Ryan. Certain ones depicted their sweet love so tenderly. Tears were flowing as I asked my aunt and mom to come and see them. Monica appeared surprised at our reaction. We were all so grateful that she shared them; based on these pictures, Ryan's last day on Earth was one of his best.

It made me wonder as a human: What would my last day of life on Earth be like before I died? I can say with clarity and gratitude that my brother had a fantastic day before leaving this place. He had the boat, cottage, and fun in town with someone who he truly loved, while also having a girlfriend up north with him to enjoy the majestic beauty together for the first time.

Now, little did I know, as the days passed, the tears fell, and the stories continued, that I would be able to channel my brother for the next two months. I think back to it now and wonder how I got through; realistically it was another burn out, but I made it!

One evening at my home, before the funeral arrangements began, my kids were sleeping, and my husband was in our kitchen cleaning the dishes.

I was present to the lights on in the kitchen, peeking in through the crack of my bedroom door. The dark felt like a warm blanket as I rested my head on my pillow. I had been lying down for a bit on my queen-sized bed. I had done so much crying that day- that being with others felt heavy on my head. I felt physically and emotionally exhausted. Suddenly, I could see a dark silhouette of Ryan's Spirit sitting at the bottom of my bed, he appeared hunched over, looking down, and he felt despondent.

I asked him, "What's the matter, Ryan?"

He shared, *I'm so disappointed and sad, I want to show you something.*

Holding space for my brother's Spirit and pain felt deep and genuine. There wasn't anything I wasn't going to do for him.

"Okay, Ry, go ahead," I replied out loud.

I closed my eyes and allowed myself to relax in the dark. In the next few moments, with my eyes still closed, I felt like I was up high. The space around me felt like I was above the ground. In my mind's eye I saw my own body shadowed and colorless. It felt like what I was seeing was happening to me. Appearing high above something, I looked down at my feet. I could see the feet clear with color. Then, as quickly as I saw them, I felt a slip of the right foot. My body felt a brief free fall, impact, and then I was surrounded in black. I didn't feel scared, it was relatively peaceful. My human mind thought, *Then what?*

As I waited, feeling blissful and nothingness all at the same time, the vision moved towards seeing myself in the van at the moment I realized, *Could it be Ryan?* Then I felt a lift from the dark. I found myself back in the driveway seeing Ryan's spirit after I just heard of his death at our childhood home.

I quickly opened my eyes and came back to my room. Overwhelmed a little by what I just saw, I asked Ryan, "Why did you show me that?"

He said, *Because it was you that brought me out of the dark. I could feel your heart feeling mine, and that's how I found you.*

How I processed that was unique. I've been seeing Spirits and experiencing the world in energy form since I was a young child. At the time, I didn't understand many things that happened to me or things I would see or feel until much later in my early twenties with the help of spiritual teachers. Honorable mention to Brenda, I might add! I had lingering fear over the years of appearing or sounding crazy.

It wasn't safe to discuss this topic for many centuries, but now we had a curious space that opened to the realm of the unseen or supernatural.

So, I pondered to myself, could that have happened to Ryan? Did he just show me how he died? Everyone's mind was being plagued by the thought of how it happened and why.

He jumped from high rocks most of his life, even when he was young; how did he fall?

Ryan had come back to show me how he fell to his death, yet I still wasn't sure if anyone believed me. For weeks, my mom, Monica, and I would get together at my home to support one another and talk for hours in the night after my kids went to bed. His Spirit would show up randomly at all different times and places. I never knew what to expect from him and he continued to surprise me.

I would see him sitting beside them, or he would sit between us; he would talk to me while I was listening to them. My mom and Monica were new to Spirit contact. So, in a way, it became an exciting experience to be part of for each of us. It became an exchange they had many questions about, and I would answer them honestly based on what I felt, saw, and heard. Most times, I heard him and witnessed his expressions in response to what we were talking about or what I was processing out loud. I would share it on his behalf to them and my dad.

It appeared to bring Ryan joy and gratitude.

Are you wondering how I saw him? Well, it was like an unmistakably clear white silhouette with bodied expressions that I saw or felt in my own body, and I could hear what he was saying in my mind, word for word. As if he was just right there, because his Spirit was.

We sat at my wooden dining room table beside my kitchen one evening. Most of the lights were out, except one just above our heads. I had made some tea for us three women and my mom took out her journal, as she loved writing things down that Ryan would share.

He asked if he could speak, and if I would share. I agreed, so I took out that journal and began writing what I heard him say. It flowed quickly; I could see where he was standing and heard him clearly in my mind like a telephone. Mom and Monica were both very taken aback; puzzled yet inspired too. One of the comments he made to his girlfriend in that channel was, *Go look for the hidden gems.* We finished another late night and pondered the different things he had shared, along with different memories or experiences we had with Ryan. It was so helpful to be together and process the many aspects of his life, even the hard ones. The evening ended very late, and we said goodnight.

Days later my mother and I got a call from Monica asking to get together as soon as we could. She had "found something". I was on the phone with her, staring out the patio door into my backyard. I pushed her for more information about what she found, but it was emotional for her, and she said it was important to be in person. I affirmed her feelings and waited patiently while we found a date that worked for us all.

Mom and I were very concerned by this; it had our minds going in many directions for days as we spoke on the phone and played the guessing game. What could it be?

Finally we met at my house, I made some hot tea, gathered around the wooden table again, and I asked her, "What is it you wanted to share with us?" There was no beating around the bush; we had to get to business.

After receiving his message to look for gems, she went through her phone and found two videos. She forgot all about the videos after the accident. The footage was not easy for her to find and watch. She showed up with great courage to share that with our family.

One video was the first jump Ryan took. Standing tall on the Canadian Shield at Raven Lake, with cedar trees to his right, pine and maple trees behind him. He took his first giant leap out; water splashed with twinkling sparkles from the sun hitting the dark blue surface. We witnessed on this video his bright, happy smile emerge from the water.

Imprinted in my mind to this day is that sheer joy on his face. Ryan was fearless when it came to jumping from tall heights; at nine years old, he jumped off a twenty-five-foot rock face into a river pool in Nova Scotia. We had been hiking and he took off without us knowing where he went and then *whoosh*, down goes Ryan into the water. He was the first of his buddies to drive a car; he was eager to take on challenging jobs that pushed his limits. He would take his snowmobile into the woods without trails and get stuck for hours and work his way out all by himself. He was overall daring, intense, and lived on the wild side.

Then there was the second video. There was a long pause as Monica pre-warned us this was the fall video, and we didn't have to watch it if we thought it would be too painful.

The morning before Ryan died, he took Monica into town, where they climbed the Dorset fire tower which overlooked miles of tree-tops and lake. They took beautiful pictures together at the tower, surrounded with cloudless sky, a beautiful sun.

They returned from town, and he wanted to take her to the jump spot by boat. In years before, we had a specific rock face that our family members and friends jumped from; even before I was old enough to walk, that was the spot. He packed himself and Monica into the large blue canoe that had a small motor on the back. For some reason that day, Ryan chose a rock face that we don't jump at; close, but I guess he was looking for something new, a challenge or thrill. When he jumped, he needed to jump out far as there was a rock sticking out under the water that he needed to clear.

Monica was left in the boat filming but also didn't know how to swim. So, after he took his first jump, she begged him not to go again, but he needed to go one last time.

My mother and I were in shock that she even found this. We were about to watch it; Mom and I waited a moment and asked ourselves if this was a good idea. We both agreed that it felt important to confirm what happened, and we decided to watch it.

It took me years to clear it from my mind, but it validated what he showed me the week or so before on my bed. We watched the slip of the right foot, his reach for trees, then the freefall, impact, and the camera's view shaking as it pointed at the water.

How brave of his girlfriend to find that, be part of re-living it, and then share it with us. We had a huge cry and supported one another through that formidable witness. When I told my dad about it and asked if he wanted to watch it, it was a hard no, and who could blame him? He was angry that I had even asked him.

I continued to imagine the first video and the smile and sparkles on the water, knowing he died doing something he absolutely loved with a woman he loved. The gifts that followed this tragic loss were incredible, but it took some of our family members years to see it that way. The details that follow are after he landed and may need some preparing before reading.

Monica was drifting away from his body and waving in the air for help, as Ryan was floating on the surface of the water for a short time, before descending deeper. He did hit his head on the way down, which explained the black out after the free fall and, then he drowned because he was unconscious from the hit. His body continued to sink.

A pontoon boat came by soon after and stopped to help Monica. First, they got her safely onto their boat. The woman on the boat was a social worker who called in the accident. She had a young man on the boat who was a diver and he quickly begun diving for Ryan's body. Ryan had become lodged in the rock that was deep where he jumped. We later counted this as a blessing because if he jumped where we usually did, he may have been too deep to find.

The young man couldn't pull him out on his own, so he called a friend on the lake that was training to be an underwater welder. Together they were both able to hold their breath long enough to pull Ryan out, then rode their boat to our cottage and the ambulance took him to the hospital from there.

What were the chances of a boat coming by at the right time, with two trained young men who could hold their breath long enough under water to get him out and the social worker who was equipped to handle the crisis? There are gifts through grief.

To me, the pieces that continued to come together after he left were mind-bending. I kept having to self-check, is this really happening? How did he know to tell her to look for something? Not sure what kind of gem that was, but it did the trick, and she found it.

I believe my credibility grew after that. As my mom would say, "I didn't believe you so much before when you spoke about seeing or hearing Spirits. But then you started seeing and hearing my son and I was determined to be open and believe." My mom's openness was pretty life-changing for me after seeing energy and Spirits all my life and never sharing it with her.

That was another gift that continued to nourish our relationship, thanks to Ryan.

Pain and loss can bring people closer in a way that may not have been possible before.

We seemed to have moved closer to what's accurate and true within ourselves versus hiding behind fears, guilt, and past hurts.

The vulnerability of loss stripped away the walls, barriers, and old beliefs and led us into new territory that we didn't see coming, to me, that became the gift.

5: Light Within My Shadows

Over the ten years before Ryan's passing, I had spontaneous visions of speaking at our family's church in front of many people. My mind would play out what I would say about my father, thinking these visions were showing me when I would lose my dad. I felt such passionate love in these visions. That evening after seeing how Ryan died, I re-interpreted the old vision; it was my brother's funeral that I was seeing, not my dad's. My dad also shared on our drive from the hospital to the cottage that he always had this intuitive gut feeling he would lose a child at a young age.

Having intuitive visions can, at times, be alarming or confusing. It's like getting certain puzzle pieces and awaiting the lost ones to bring it all together. I've learned over time to trust that I will receive further guidance when I need to know, and I remain open to the guidance along the way, as the unknown can have us all shake in our pants sometimes.

The funeral approached. I attempted to prepare the speech that I volunteered to do. That day my friend/sister Erin—by spirit and choice—arrived at my home. I updated her on my progress and requested her help. Writing felt like a substantial task, and I was stuck.

My relationship with Erin is unique and special. There is an energetic tone to how we communicate and exchange together. It usually takes us some moments to find energy balance when we first share space. We used to laugh as we both activated each other when together, and it could feel overwhelming or awkward in the body. But we soon settled into ease and connection. Erin was very close to Ryan; he felt safe and cared for by her. For him to share himself vulnerably said a lot about the person's spirit and nature.

I had tried to write this obituary a couple times with no luck. It all sounded generic, and I wasn't feeling the passionate heart that my visions had. Erin suggested we go into the back yard together.

The sun was sparkling through the ninety-three-year-old silver maple tree, which I named "Grandma Mabel" after my father's mom. We sat on a blanket and the air was warm and calming.

I had been discussing song options to sing at his funeral with Erin a couple days before. In high school, myself, Erin's mother Eileen, and our other sister-friend Alicia, sang together at our family's Catholic church. With Erin's eloquent taste in music, she suggested a beautiful tune called *Angel Band* by The Peasall Sisters. What a number, and it was approved by the church too!

While under the tree, Erin and I sang *Amazing Grace* together to get inspired. This song was sung at my grandmother Mabel's funeral, and it is dear to my father's family. We harmonized in a way that melded our souls together; each note with its beautiful vibrations connected us to nature and that moment. I closed my eyes and let the harmonics swirl around us; I felt present in the center of my heart.

Then the fun! It was like I was part of a triangle with Erin and Ryan. Spirit truly can work in mysterious ways. We connected, and messages just bounced back and forth from me to her, and so on. We were both present to the synergy of this triangle, and before we knew it, we had a whole page and a half. It was completed with excitement and amazement; little did we know this message would touch so many in such profound ways. I couldn't believe I was part of it.

She picked me up the day of the funeral, as she said, "No one should be driving themselves to their brother's funeral." Then, with Sigur Rós playing over the speakers and tears flowing, we prepared ourselves energetically and emotionally for what was about to occur.

I felt drained from the day before; Ryan's wake was overwhelmingly large. For four hours straight, people lined up outside of the funeral home to come to greet our family. It took our family by surprise to see how many people his life impacted.

It was a strange feeling being the family members that everyone looked at with many emotions, for us and themselves, at the funeral. I kept strong for my kids and my parents. I walked up with my paper when it was time to share my speech. Addressing all beliefs and connections to a higher source felt good to do in the Catholic church. I struggled growing up; I didn't resonate wholeheartedly. I hold trust and compassion for what anyone chooses for them. For me, nature and the elements are where I find my connection to Source.

The words rolled off my tongue with distinction. I wasn't shaky; I was so clear. Not a single tear—well maybe a little choke-up when I spoke about Monica. I looked into the eyes of everyone in the room as I shared the truth and message of unconditional divine love. I'm forever grateful for that whole experience and all those who approached and touched my spirit after.

With the speech done, our quartet later sang *Amazing Grace*, and I almost cried but held my composure. We followed with the Angel Band song, a four-part harmony with Eileen on the guitar in the church choir loft. It was such an honor singing with those three women. I sung my heart out, and on the last note, I turned it into an *om* and fell to my knees weeping. That moment began the growing evolution of my mediumship messages with Ryan.

Erin came over to me, giving me reiki above my head. My husband ran up from the pew and sat on my right side, rubbing my back. My three-year-old son was calling, "Mama, where's Mama?" and my good-friend Beki ran up and held space at my feet; nothing was stopping her from helping.

Then I saw my brother standing behind Erin as I released tears and breathed deeply. I could see light flowing through each one of us and back into each other from him.

It created the shape of the infinity sign.

I calmed down, feeling the overwhelming comfort of Ryan's presence. I looked up at him, smiling, and he said, *I am the new Jesus* with an enthusiastic tone. Ryan was witty and very funny.

It made me laugh inside. I was not ready to share what I saw or heard just yet, as I didn't know what people would think or if they would even believe me. I hardly believed it myself.

We settled and finished the funeral. The priest gave such a beautiful, honest share, as he knew my parents well. Everyone gathered at the Knights of Columbus Hall next.

To describe what it felt like to be in the spotlight after reading channeled speech is hard to put into words. So many people came to me with the purity of their hearts and thanked me, sharing how it touched them. I became a magnet for so many people who shared their hearts openly. I was a bit overwhelmed and grateful, yet I forwarded the credit to Ryan and the mystery of Spirit that created the messages; I was just the messenger.

As a Reiki Master Practitioner for almost fourteen years now, I honor the chi, or universal energy, that flows through to provide healing. I am but a vessel that holds space openly, like during my experience at Ryan's funeral.

To be in that channel was a great gift, for love is all God/Creator/Oneness.

When I stood in a place of love, there often was an abundance of blessings that flowed. Being open to receiving how they came to me was one of the biggest lessons I am here on Earth to learn.

I was not the only one who experienced communication with Ryan that day. The night of the funeral, my mom and I snuggled with my three-year-old son in bed.

Lying down between us looking up, he said to us, "I saw Wyan, Mom."

Coming as a surprise and shock, we asked, "What did you say?"

"I saw Uncle Wyan at dat place."

I asked, "At the church today?"

"Yes dere," he said. "He went dis way, den dat way, den dis way, den dat way, again n' again," while he turned his head left and right over and over in the bed.

I looked at my mom with wide eyes, and we listened some more.

"Den his eyes did dis, den dat, open, close, open close," while he blinked his eyes wide open and closed.

From my experience and guidance from teachers, listening to kids at a young age and acknowledging their spirit encounters is vital in learning to trust their abilities.

"How did it feel, was it good to see him?" I asked.

"Yup, dis way, den dat way," he continued.

"Thank you for sharing buddy, he was visiting you," I concluded. Then I snuggled him to sleep while Mom and I reveled in the moment and all he shared.

My father didn't enjoy connecting with Spirits unless it was his grandfather showing up on the roads while driving his motorcycle. When you lose a son, though, I guess openness can occur because three days after Ryan left, my dad sensed someone stepping into the room while he was lying down. While resting in bed at home, he looked down at the foot of the bed; there was a little boy. It was Ryan staring right at him, showing himself as a young boy. Dad felt very emotional but welcomed the encounter, as he desperately wanted to feel close to his son again.

You never know when your life will take a turn, whether it be death, birth, sickness, health, an accident, near-end, heartbreak, burnout, psychic awakening, or mediumship with Spirits.

I firmly believe that when you are ready for your next challenge, experience, or phase of life, it finds you. All you need to do is show up, do your best, and surrender to the process.

The healing road of grief is unique and painful, and there is no measure of time to expect it will be over; it's a long road of ups and downs that is not linear. Some days it felt better while others snuck right up and kicked me in the face. I was surprised by the weeks that followed as a medium between this world and the one he just arrived in.

I struggled for a whole week and many months after the funeral with this one specific regret that turned into anger. As I shared before, when I saw Ryan's body in the hospital, I realized I didn't get that one last hug when he showed up for bed sheets at Nanny's apartment.

It still creates tears in my eyes thinking about it; this one regret took so long to let go of.

We never truly know when our last moments with someone will be; this perspective now guides me into presence. I find courage to share my true feelings and I try not to stay upset with people for too long appreciating the life we share together or how it may serve us both.

Presence is a powerful gateway and goal to build with. Many relationships or experiences trigger emotion, thought, resistance, or ideas that either take me from the present moment or move me towards it. It's always my choice; awareness of this has become critical.

Many emotions led up to the funeral, the shock of his death took years to lessen, and life slowed down a little after the funeral passed, which felt like another death process. The hype was over, people went home, and there I was with all my layers, regrets, and emotions. It felt like a high and the low that followed was something I learned to hold myself through.

Over the next month, my family members were troopers. My husband learned a lot of what my job truly entailed, being a mother of two spiritually aware boys and managing a home. I give thanks every day for his courage, heart, and commitment to us. This grief journey indeed offered him gifts he didn't see coming either and prepared him for his grief journey only a couple of years later with the loss of his mom.

Have you ever played something back in your head over and over, hoping it could have been different? You are not alone; it's more common than I think we talk about.

I reflected on that moment at my Nannys', when Ryan arrived to borrow bedsheets the day before he left for the cottage with Monica. I heard his voice and felt that pull to hug him, but I didn't. I had missed my last chance before he died, not knowing. I had to let myself heal slowly before letting that one go, it felt like huge guilt and regret.

In the past, I felt that letting go needed to happen quickly after an experience. *Come on already, get over it,* said an old voice in my head. I knew that healing was up and down and not linear. One layer led into the next; grief and regret brought our family into presence together as we faced the hard parts of letting things go.

No matter what I'm facing, healing takes time. It can feel like a big pain in my ass but as it passes, I see the value and in time perspective shifts and I change some more.

I moved forward some, then back. I felt peace, then anger. It was like the waves of the ocean that somehow moved me where I needed to be just by going with the flow of each layer.

After months of many tears and release, I forgave myself for not getting up that day at Nanny's; in this forgiveness, warmth came in and helped me through.

Years later, more regrets resurfaced to process, like how I wasn't there more in Ryan's darkest hours, how could I have been kinder as a kid, how I contributed to his struggles. I regret not telling him more how proud I was of how far he came in his last year of life after all he'd been through. I regretted all the times I kept my distance when it felt hard to connect with him. I regretted the boundaries I set when he was coming out of active addiction, because I had no trust left.

If I let it, that list could have grown exponentially big, and I would have made myself ill over it. After a while of naming the regrets and letting myself cry or talk them out, I chose to see the good I did share. I chose to remember the ways that I was there for him, the opportunities of connection we did exchange. All the moments when he let me in made a difference for him. I kept those close to my heart and remembered the good.

I will be honest, I used to get really upset that I could only remember the darker times or struggles. I used to reach and push myself to remember the good memories. In time, as I processed and healed through the dark, I was able to remember more of the good. Being together with family, Monica and Ryan's friends helped as people shared stories of him and we got to hear of different sides of him that others got to see.

Often family gets the hard parts of being with each other and when out in the world, we share our best. That's what family is for, the good, the bad and the ugly. It's unconditional love that provides a safe place to land, fall apart, pick back up and create a new with. I'm not saying our family didn't have conditions or struggles in accepting the difficulty, but when push came to shove, we returned to unconditional by trying to own our own shit and listen with compassion, because we love each other.

Death has a way of bringing things to the surface that we perhaps wouldn't or couldn't deal with while someone's still alive. Family meetings in the past were funny and annoying as we are all sensitive humans. Ryan hated those moments when we got the call from my parents: "Come on down its time to talk." We would gather on the couches of our family's living room and Ryan would be the furthest away, turned looking into another room. With all that he carried, the guilt, the pressure and the lack of coping strategies, his reaction is understandable today.

There were things I didn't say, and things Ryan and I didn't get to process together and that hurt more after he was gone. There were things we didn't get to do together and milestones my parents wouldn't witness. Grief helped me to re-evaluate my life, my choices, relationships, and much more. Showing up in that honest way felt like too much at first, but with slow surrender it served our lives very well.

There are many ways that our family healed from this. I acknowledge and applaud the courage it took to look into ourselves, our choices and to keep choosing presence, love, and life together after he left.

What I learned most was to live each day with that same courage and tell people in my life when I'm feeling proud of them. I let people know how they can support me as I learn what I need. I ask others what they need so I can show up for them too, or be honest when I don't have the capacity.

I learned that I need space often to stay in my own lane so that I can differentiate what energy is mine and process it before coming to others with important exchanges. That will be a work in progress and one of my most important practices.

With grief, regret, and pain there came perspective, healing, and connection. Being brave and willing to surrender to the process made that possible.

6: Death on the Dream Farm

I have been journaling since I was a young girl. I don't remember anyone ever telling me to journal; I just felt innately drawn to the practice. Energy, to me, could feel like a volcanic eruption or a heavy burden as an empathetic person. Sometimes it could feel like surging energy all over without a clear avenue to channel it. Journaling brought me peace and helped clarify my feelings, thoughts, and sensations. In my experience, journaling is a sacred union with self, Spirit, Creator, God, or a higher power of my knowing.

One night, soon after Ryan had died, Brandon and I had an honest talk in the warm glowing light of our living room. We were cozy on our brown leather couch, and I expressed how powerful feelings had been emerging for me through writing, which led me to take out my nine journals to show him. I had them stored in a Rubbermaid bin in our attic; I took them out and stacked them all high on the wooden coffee table. I had filled them with detailed dreams, expressions from my school years, hard break-ups with boyfriends, channeled poems, and deep ponderings about life. They all offered some reflection into my spiritual and human evolution, and I'm glad I kept them.

To my surprise that night with Brandon, I found a dream journal entry from July of 2016, almost two months before Ryan's passing. This dream struck me as synchronistic, and the timing of it surprised me.

The dream began with me walking through an old farmhouse with high walls and old wood-framed doorways. It seemed to me like a gathering. There were many people dressed in black walking around this home. I was pulled towards a room where I could partially see a body lying face-up on a dining room table.

The room was simple and most of the furniture was wooden. As I moved into the room, I saw it was a dead body lying on the table. I realized I was at a funeral, and sensed male energy from the body.

I couldn't get close enough to see a face, though I tried. I felt a deep sadness all around me. I turned to leave the room and walked through the kitchen, where several family members solemnly gathered. I walked through the people to the back door, then I left the house and walked into the long, tall grass. In the distance, I saw a large paddock with horses grazing in the field. I walked up to an old wooden fence and watched them.

I felt peaceful and continued to gaze at the horses with admiration. I was inspired to walk under the fence into the field and began dancing with the horses with my arms stretched out, and I felt free. Then I woke up.

Exploring the dream analogy to me is like meditation. I've been practicing for over twenty years, remembering, discussing, documenting, and finding hidden messages that guide my life. I took this dream and explored what it meant to me; I dreamt of an old farmhouse representing my family's home where we gathered after he died. *Dead on the table* was how I saw him at the hospital after his accident. People dressed in black signified the funeral and gathering. Watching the *horses* was the freedom and grace that came from healing through loss. The horses represented change, stamina, and spirit guides. The *herd* of horses represented the family. I've known since I was a young child that I wanted to own a horse and have a farm. Being a lot older now I also know how much work is needed for that task, so I'm open to how that experience may turn out for me this time around the sun.

I was surprised and amazed by this dream, Brandon and I had just spoke about journaling, which guided me towards finding this dream. I felt very affirmed by the power of this dream, because two months later, Ryan passed away, we gathered in the old century home and through healing grief, it led me to inner freedom.

As expressed before, receiving validation can strengthen trust with the universe and our internal guidance system. Growing trust in my intuition continued to grow through these experiences with Ryan. The dream boosted my confidence. Validations such as these, grounded my trust in listening and following through.

This first validation—how he died—was quite a lot to take in, but this dream felt a little lighter.

As time passed, I moved through the fear of appearing crazy, because it wasn't a fact; it was the fear of being wrong or judged. Fear for me is False Evidence Appearing Real. Insanity is trying to do the same thing over and over and expect a different result, which was not the case here. I have learned over the years and with the help of cognitive behavioral therapy that I can challenge my thoughts and beliefs and look for the evidence that usually helps bring me back to a grounded view of the whole picture.

I challenged the old belief of "crazy" by trusting Ryan and myself; over time the voice of fear became quieter. I began talking to myself through the old thoughts and had courage to share what I was experiencing. That made a huge difference—being open about it. It's now six years later and over time of redirecting old thoughts and habits the new ones have become more of an automatic habit. I am experiencing less pushback or resistance when noticing the old beliefs.

Life is mysterious and quite magical when we wake up to the synchronicities of the universe! Energy is shifting and bouncing from objects, people, events, and experiences. There are endless cycles of evolutionary change happening around us every day. When my heart and mind became open, it became possible to explore and experience more truth and alignment.

I learned to embrace the opportunity of loss, struggle, and contrast, and let it guide me into clarity, healing and growth.

Validation can come from anywhere; it could be someone saying something that aligns perfectly with what you were talking about to someone else the day before. It could be a book that jumped out at the store with all the answers to the questions you've been asking yourself. It could be a symbol in a dream, a random occurrence related to your inquiry, or an indirect message coming from someone else that resonates with what you need.

Dreams guide me through life; they warn me of dangers and offer clues to upcoming events or possibilities. Dreams provide me with profound symbols relating to my relationships with others, myself, or subconscious habits that require further awareness or clarity. Most times the people in my dreams are representations of myself for me to explore. Other times my dreams offer messages for others or warn me about others. I've had dreams offer suggestions for my well-being that I've integrated or steered away from that were a benefit.

My brother was only beginning to look inward into his intuitive abilities in the last year of his life. He shared with my dad only a month before leaving, walking in our old neighborhood together, "I think I am a lot like Ashley, Dad."

After ten years of active addiction, masking traumas of bullying, growing up with ADHD and being a highly sensitive kid, Ryan began discovering there was more to his sensitivities than he realized.

In our family, I braved being open to new possibilities, investing years and money into learning and expanding emotionally, physically, and spiritually. I believe as I became grounded in my changes, it offered permission for Ryan to begin seeing himself differently over time. One beautiful example of how we can heal together. Unfortunately, the clarity for him began close to his death.

I went away for university in Australia in 2009 for a year and then moved to British Columbia with a partner upon returning. Ryan and I didn't get a lot of time to connect and exchange through those years. I remember being on a camping trip out west, surrounded by acres and acres of trees, where we camped at a small lake. I drove to a pay phone under a wooden-roofed structure to call Ryan, as I just felt I needed to reach him that day. Surrounded by mountains, trees, and fresh air, it was the first time we had really connected in years. He was telling me about things he would like to do, places he wanted to travel, ideas with friends, but lacked the organization and courage to do any of it. It began our relationship back to one another, as I was a safe person to process some of these things with. I was encouraging him to come out and visit me, but he never did.

When I moved home from BC, I got a chance to re-kindle my connection with Ryan. The heart-to-hearts we were able to have in person felt cleansing, meaningful, and important to me. Watching him become an uncle and how gentle and kind he became with my boys was a gift. Perhaps you have someone in your life that showed you a different way or helped you feel less alone by sharing or being who they are.

Some people call it psychic; I like to refer to myself as intuitive, less of a trigger word for me. We all can be intuitive; some of us tune in more than others. For some it flows naturally, while others learn to craft it over time. Intuition and empathy, to me, go hand in hand. They each lean on each other to work as a team.

When you come close to me, my body gives me warnings, clues or sensations in response to the energy you share or carry. To me those are empathic and intuitive abilities at work, while also the intelligence of the nervous system communicating with me too.

When you begin sharing things with me, I can see in my mind's eye different colors or impressions. At times I can hear phrases or words drop into my mind that are relevant to what you're sharing, or they may offer some deeper reflection and aid. I decided, with help from my spiritual coach, when I need to turn this down or off, so I can be present as an observer and a human experiencing. In this way I hold myself and enjoy the exchange in the moments.

While other times, I allow openness to the energies that can offer guidance, recognition of the energy present, and share with others if they would like to hear what I am picking up.

Sometimes I can sense through my body where you feel pain or stuck energy. I used to work at a small-town restaurant on the weekends when I moved home from British Columbia. At that time, I needed to begin slowly integrating back into work to strengthen my spirit and body. It was a busy breakfast spot; one afternoon this man came in through the front door of the store.

I was standing at the cash register across from him and as soon as I saw him enter, I felt a huge wave hit my heart and I felt pain inside my chest. As I smiled and greeted him, we talked very briefly after he ordered food. In that moment of being open to what he was feeling, he opened right up and told me that he was having a bad day as his wife was leaving him. I shared some compassion and kind energy, took his money, and off he went with the sandwich he ordered.

A lot of times, all throughout my life, strangers or people I hardly know spill their lives out to me, and I never understood why. This has taught me the fine balance between being open and protective of my energy while honoring the sacred exchanges with people's spirits.

Often I can see stagnant or dense energy or shades of color around people that are missing healthy glow, which I leave as an observation and send off a prayer their way. I respect that people will feel called to come work together with me and what I see is not my business, but to redirect into prayer or kind intention.

Sometimes I can hear in my mind what people are about to say before it's said. When the phone rings I hear a name or sense the energy of the person calling.

When I'm in my Reiki practice, my intuition guides my hands to where there are blocks in people's bodies or energy fields. I also hear or sense visual impressions and symbols to help identify past connections to these blocks, clues to past events and feelings, or helpful avenues to grow forward with as Reiki energy clears it out.

As stated above, I've learned to live a sane life by turning it down or closing off when I need. In this way I visualize a light dimming or being turned right off, along with a prayer. This helps me get into my own energy and lane letting any energy that arises to just keep passing me by.

I don't search into people's energy, unless you are on my Reiki table, and you have asked me to. I respect and hold true to having people's permission and if ever I've crossed a boundary, I practice coming to the exchange with integrity and willingness to heal my part.

I have learned to use the elements and nature to process and release energy that accumulates being around or helping others. Everything is energy and entering the flows of joy or hardship with conscious intent, acceptance, and trust with nature has become a new resource for me to cope and continue healing work.

Walking the road of an intuitive may sound fun; at times it can be quite exhausting. Which is why I've burnt out so many times and I still practice the balance between helping and restoring. If I bring you back to the synchronicities of this experience with my brother, there were so many moments that clicked as if a higher intelligence was at work.

I believe life is full of meaningful coincidences that synchronize moments between two or more people. Therefore, bringing together unrelated or unplanned events that relate. Meaning and purpose find and guide humans in a way we can't always explain.

Approximately five years before he got the job as a custodian, Ryan and I prepared for his interview. He was full of anxiety and wasn't sure if he would get through it. So, we practiced together; I gave him some helpful pointers, such as pausing for a breath before answering or talking less and being intentional with his answers. It was at that moment in the small little computer room of our century home that I planted a seed of change. I shared with him to make lasting change; we need to walk through the trenches of mud, muck and mess of our lives to get to the root of pain, to move towards the good and proud. With all my heart, I told him it was worth every bit of struggle or sacrifice; he wasn't alone, I had my own too.

He did the interview, was an anxious ball and slipped up many times, but a woman who approached me after his funeral said they saw his potential and she said to me, "Anyone who can survive working at a mushroom farm for four years has what it takes for the job," and he was hired.

He met Monica in one of the schools he worked at two years before he died. My family and I truly believe it was their long slow courting and falling in love that helped him shift from the inside out. We are forever grateful for that opportunity and for Monica.

A couple months before he died, he called me three times; phone calls were very rare between us. Communicating with words was a real challenge for him at times. He had anxiety and a social phobia but understanding the sensitivity and empathy was a lot to handle. Then, rare times, he would be in the zone; funny, interactive, and his true self. I loved those moments.

On the phone, he shared how he couldn't go on another night without sleep, almost breaking down into tears. My dad believed he was trying to adjust to some medication to help with anxiety, and he silently suffered at night not letting anyone in on his struggles. I didn't know what he was suffering from; he was so tired and caught up in his mind but wouldn't let me in any further. He later shared with my dad he thought he was losing his mind in the basement most nights. I asked him to reach out after work and told him that I was there for him. I was just so grateful he was reaching out to me. He didn't call back or come by; visits and communication had to work on his terms. I waited patiently.

I got the opportunity to share with him honestly and help in those three phone calls with what he was open to share. Most specifically, I remember talking about *The Control Dramas from Celestine Prophecy* by James Redfield. The third time he called, he asked me about them again; these helped him place the energy struggles in certain relationships, which led him to reflect on how sensitive he was to others.

A week before he died, he called asking if we could talk to our father together. He was ready to share some of his truths with some support; this was a big moment for me as his sister. I was so ready to be at his side and see him stand in his truth. We had an upcoming roof job at my house; all my brothers were coming along with my dad. Ryan wanted to be clear of his needs and intentions before the job began. Big shift for boundaries!

So, while Ryan and my dad drove by to visit, I began the conversation with my dad on my driveway, then Ryan opened the gate and came out from the back of the yard and stepped in.

I witnessed him take a big breath and he began sharing.

My dad listened and respected his needs and words, and I could feel Ryan just vibrating, a significant step forward for him, honoring his need to be seen, heard, and respected.

The day before, he left for the cottage, never to return. Ryan had an opportunity to work together with his two older half-brothers and our father on a renovation on the upper floor of our family home. If you know these incredible men, they are full of stubborn jam, hot-headed passion, and strong hearts and hands. Although this wasn't the roof job, they needed to be a very present team to get the flooring done. The bedroom had many uneven challenges. It became an opportunity to let go of negativity, release control, and work through challenges with heart, teamwork, and fun. It was a synchronistic divine job that brought them all very close one last time. My heart swells with joy to know they all had this chance; my second regret is that I wasn't there too.

The day before Ryan's accident, he had a significant moment with his girlfriend. He was lying in her lap on the couch in the large screened-in porch overlooking the bay and property of our cottage. He opened vulnerably and shared his hurt from bullying when he was young. Her response was so compassionate and kind; she couldn't believe anyone would treat someone as kind as him like that. Then he wept in her lap. It must have been so healing for him to be received with such love and kindness after opening about the bullying. When I sit here writing this, it still amazes me all that lined up for him before his time was up. I am so proud of my brother and our family for risking being vulnerable, facing each other with heart, and learning to grow in uncomfortable places.

My close friend Tanya organized a Woman's Gathering to support me after the funeral. I am shifting back to the second week after he died but details help. I took off from my parents' that day with a tender heart in his small light grey Ford truck, disassociated from my kids and family. I was in such deep grief after the funeral that I needed space to process everything inside me. The windows were down, the music was flowing, and I was headed north on Highway 35. All that surrounded me was fields, the sun setting on the horizon, and homes along large properties. The truck became a sacred refuge where I could cry, sing, wail, sit, be silent, think, or talk with Ryan.

I pulled into Tanya's gravel driveway, tall trees all around her home. I grabbed some wood out of the truck for a fire and saw a vast circle of women waiting for me. Some women I'd known from elementary school and some new ones from our homeschool group. I felt such tender kindness from the group, how grateful and resistant to the support I felt.

Tanya had prepared a reading that touched us all; we shared a group smudge, and people took turns sharing from their hearts. I felt so loved, held, and heard even though I didn't say much. I've learned that it truly does take a village to raise our kids, to heal powerfully, and to evolve in this world.

Community in my opinion and experience has provided visceral webbing that I can count on to hold and guide me. Our children grew up with a community of like-minded families and together our friendships supported one another through grief, loss, celebration and so much more. I believe this is the way of creating a healthy future, so if you're in grief find a group, a community, and some kind of support you can grow together with. It may feel hard, perhaps impossible but trust in your guidance system to lead the way and ask for help getting there.

Following the circle, Ryan showed up and guided me to gather the women in a tall-tented structure on Tanya's property. Surrounded by beautiful forest, the weather was cool and comfortable. Ryan asked me to lead us in a meditation, tight side by side to bring our hearts and light together. He also wanted to connect with a couple of the women and pass on a message through them. I asked the group for permission and then began speaking with effortless flow, even though on the inside I felt so tender. It afforded me a boost of energy for the task. Ryan guided and helped with feelings of fearlessness, strength, and capability.

After the reflection, we paused in silence for him to connect; I advised those who felt a prompt in their body or mind or felt his energy to speak out. Ryan reached a few of the women. Liza, was my close friend from high school and had a warm connection with Ryan felt him first. Tanya became overcome by his presence, following a rush of adrenalin and energy; she felt like she was on the edge of a cliff. We listened to each woman with acceptance and love, being witness to Ryan's messages through woman that had not had an experience like this before.

Ryan finished off with Monice, Tanya's sister. She quietly began to feel Ryan inside her body sensationally but fearful to share and overwhelmed with the group, she remained quiet.

I was then prompted intuitively to speak.

"I know that he's inside someone, please speak up," I said compassionately.

Monice struggled to comprehend what she was experiencing and confronted the discomfort within her about speaking in a group. I looked up at her and I could see Ryan's spirit standing behind her. I could sense her hesitation so, I gave a gentle nudge to her that it was okay to share.

She thought, *Oh shit*, and she described this voice flowing in instantly; she began talking.

"I am the trees; I am the wind. I am happy and good. When you feel the wind it's my smile."

She felt everything in that moment was circular around us and Ryan was inside of our woman's circle holding space.

When we completed the circle, we hugged closely and celebrated coming together.

What a decisive moment I will never forget.

Before leaving, Monice came to me and asked, "How did you know he picked me?"

I said, "Because he was standing right behind you."

She was shocked; we hugged and smiled at each other. Monice shared recently that that was one of the most memorable moments of her life. Ryan had a thing for Monice years before, so it was sweet that he chose her to connect with.

From my experience, I've learned we don't have to be a spirit medium to receive messages from passed loved ones or have intuitive abilities to be guided by the universe.

We can experience this fascinating connection when we decide we are open and available.

It's always up to us to choose how we would like to interact or receive from the mysteries of life and the unseen.

It may just surprise you how validating it can be to receive messages or awaken to the synchronistic connections all around you. Curious exploration can become an adventure of self-discovery that brings people closer together. Bringing our innate nature into alignment with source energy. Through nature, relationships, lessons, and experiences, we are living beings with intelligent innate systems connected to everything.

Whichever is true and real for you let it guide you towards connection and purpose.

7: Living Two Worlds

Let's explore this a bit; what is Mediumship? To me it's the link between the world we live in and the supernatural or unseen world. It's a channel of communication that comes through many senses beyond the five main ones we learn about. Through these heightened senses I pick up energies, information, and impressions that help myself or other humans receive messages. The messages or impressions are often helpful or healing for loved ones.

At times, the help and healing connects us to those that have passed away too. For example, when I healed parts of the generational experience of shame and silence, that energy flowed to my ancestors too.

As a young person, when I saw my first strange holographic face come out of the wall, I didn't know what to think other than fear. The basement was a scary place, not because it was dark, but because I could feel the energy of a man from our furnace room. The dark was just a reminder that I may not see things clearly or be ready for what I would see.

The basement of our home used to be an apartment where we had a couple of different tenants. There were three tiny windows, so it didn't have much light. There were a couple small rooms that my dad built that Ryan, and I stayed in at different times as we grew up.

As Mediumship and Empathic sensitivities increased, I believe as a young child I felt danger in being open, so I tried to close off to protect myself. I often felt confused and overwhelmed by the emotion of others. Spirit contact felt even sharper and more intense in my body. When I saw heavy clouds around people's bodies or felt overwhelming sensations from certain objects, people, or places, I tried to shut it out and ignore it.

This created the feeling of living two worlds and trying to navigate them wherever I went without being aware of why. As I grew older my experiences changed as I lived and learned, which helped me to open with grounded perspective when contacting spirits or reading energies. I'm grateful for my experiences as they shaped who I am today. Lessons were overwhelming and scary at times, yet somehow the universe guided my path to helpers, relationships that healed and teachers that made sense of my experiences. Have faith and trust in your path too!

When I was in high school, I got mononucleosis.

I slept hours day and night at first, tired all the time and had to be home schooled by one of my teachers and I couldn't hang out with friends for almost six months. That was a very isolated time in my life, which I was familiar with, but didn't make it any easier to cope.

While sick, I had a moment which to this day I am not sure if I was dying or was the beginning of an out of body experience. It felt like the energy or essence of my being was lifting from my physical body and I was aware of it. My body was completely heavy and still and I couldn't move, I began crying and saying out loud, "I don't want to die or leave."

My Spirit body felt like it had begun lifting my consciousness and I kept crying asking it to come back. It dropped back into my body after what felt like fifteen minutes and wiping my tears I went back to sleep; told no one about it. It's fair to say I was very depressed through that sickness period but I healed and persevered.

After university in Australia, I lived in British Columbia where I lived in an old century home with my partner at the time and a friend for almost a year. The walls were tall with a deep yellow paint and crown molding; it was beautiful, with large windows and plenty of rooms on the second floor. We got a tour of the place from a friend who bought it as an investment home to rent. While we took time to decide on the lease, I walked into the third bedroom and instantly felt a young energy in the closet. As I got closer, I saw in my mind's eye, it was a young girl with long brown hair who felt shy and afraid of me.

Throughout our time living there, she would come out to explore; I'd see her body standing in the doorway of our living room as I was cutting resources for the daycare program I supervised. That was the second time I saw with my two eyes, first time was the male Spirit in my basement, but she was a white translucent body, something you would see in the movies. She continued having encounters with me throughout our stay there.

One night, I lay on my bed in the bedroom up halfway from where she usually lingered. I sensed her come in the doorway, and then saw indents push into my bed like she was crawling on the bed towards me and came right into my face. I got so spooked because I was seeing it with my two eyes not my mind's eye that I quickly closed my eyes and said, "Love and light, love and light, love and light," and she got scared away and was gone when I opened my eyes.

Another night, I was almost asleep in my bed. As I drifted off, I instantly saw her take my hand and move it towards an old telephone on a side table beside where my bed was. I picked it up in my sleep state and saw her standing in front of me with a knife like she had been hurt. This woke me up from sleep and I looked around to see her and she was gone. I wondered if this was her way of showing me what happened to her.

The last encounter, I was asleep in my bed, in what felt like half a dream state as it felt so real. I stood in the bathroom that had a huge narrow window, tall ceiling, tiles on the floor and a standalone tub like you would see in the old days. I heard her scream and I tried to scream to wake myself up.

I couldn't move from the bathroom. Filled with fear, I kept trying to push a scream out, and then I woke up. At this point I had to close off from her so I could focus on my waking life, and we moved soon after. This time of my life was heavy and confusing personally so I can see now that the lack of grounding, managing pain while working, waiting for knee surgery and having uncertain encounters was overwhelming and may have contributed to the fear.

Feeling and sensing energy had many avenues for me, each time I got pregnant I felt my child's Spirit come through me at conception. We conceived Jack after Brandon's grandfather's funeral; I was not prepared to be a mother and it was not a conscious act. I had just gotten off birth control pills a month before, after taking them for just under ten years.

As our hearts intimately came together after the funeral of his Pa, I felt a consciousness come into my body. Which was confirmed a couple of weeks later when I took a test and was pregnant.

When we conceived Ben, it was intentional. As that intimacy took place, I witnessed the top half of a male body with long braided hair hovering above Brandon in the room which then descended into my body. A couple of weeks later I was pregnant with our second child. It felt like such an honor to be present to their souls as they came into life, in my body.

I told Brandon later; although he did not understand my experience, he offered a generous heart and listened to me. He continues today to offer that openness when I share my spiritual experiences, for that I'm grateful. In time with his openness, it helped him see different perspectives with a willing heart and see that two worlds can indeed exist together.

I traveled to Nova Scotia when our kids were two and four years old, with my dad, mom, and grandparents; Brandon stayed home to work. On the trip, my mom and I went out to a tavern for some music one night. We didn't get a lot of time, just the two of us, so this was a treat. There was a gentleman that sent two drinks over to us from the bar.

I asked the waitress who it was from, and he waved at us. After a while of listening to live music, I went to the washroom and thanked the gentleman upon passing.

He appeared kind enough, as I wanted to check in with his intention and we met him later at another tavern. As the evening went on my mother grew tired and wanted to leave to go to bed; she was not happy with me that I was staying but I let her know I would be okay and to trust me, as our home was just a block away.

Later the gentleman and I left the tavern and walked a couple blocks to the harbor before saying goodbye for the night. This town had one main road that lined the ocean. It was dark but there were lights along the pier of the harbor, and we found a spot to sit where we talked, and he shared about losing his girlfriend to cancer recently.

In that short moment, there was her Spirit, sitting at the pier with us beside him.

I saw her long blond hair and certain details of her face. I told him what I saw, and he was very taken back by this. He walked me home, I said thank you for meeting us and maybe I will see you around town.

We visited for two weeks; one evening I was sitting outside watching the stars at night and the girlfriend's Spirit arrived by my side. I was sitting at a picnic table at the back of the house we rented, my kids fast asleep, taking in the stars. She asked me if I could give him a message.

So, I went inside, found paper and a pen, and wrote down what I heard her say. I looked for the gentleman periodically whenever I went and never found him.

I had this little note from her and clear quartz crystal I used when connected with her to give him. It wasn't until the last evening, when I was driving back to the house that I saw him walking along the main road on the sidewalk.

I chuckled to myself; the synchronicity was outstanding, and I learned trust in the universe through that experience. I pulled over, rolled my window down and said, "Hey, I have something for you."

I passed him the note and crystal and thanked him for our encounter, and he thanked me too. We stayed in touch, as grief became something we both related to after Ryan died.

Sometimes I don't get all the details at once; it's the fun part of trusting and leaning into the mysteries of spiritual experiences. Which brings me to my last example of living two worlds.

I was at my friend's house for a party, when I got a call from a young person whom I know well. She called late in the night and sounded anxious and worried. Her and some girlfriends had some explorative fun with a Ouija board. I answered and listened. They had called out a young boy leaving them all scared and unsure about what to do. I could sense there was some partying going on and encouraged them to avoid mixing the two, and quite honestly avoid the Ouija board altogether.

I offered some grounded support aloud on the speaker phone, gave them some instructions as a group to anchor in their energies and help the boy's Spirit. She thanked me and we said goodbye.

Now months later, I was in my youngest son's room giving him a cuddle for bed. He was a little unsettled in his room and felt uneasy. He asked me to check his room for "visitors," as we call Spirits. I tuned into his room energetically and the young boy from that night with the girls showed up at the bottom of his bed. I knew instantly and intuitively it was the boy. I asked him if he wanted help, to which he agreed. I imagined a green candlelight and asked him to move towards it and trust that he would be okay. I held the intention and energy with him until he slipped right through the light, and all was complete.

After Ryan's death, I began to feel like I was living in two worlds; one foot in this world but I was barely present to it. The other foot was in the unseen Spirit world, which was exciting, curious, and comforting because it brought me closer to Ryan. It was spontaneous when Ryan checked in; he visited my oldest son at school within the first month of his passing too.

One day, my son came home and said, "Mom, Uncle Ryan was at school today."

I was inquisitive and asked, "Wow, he came to visit you; what was that like?"

He shared, "I was writing, he came over, touched my arm and helped me write my letters. His hand was cold on my arm." He pointed with his little finger where Ryan had touched him.

I was in awe that this was happening to my kids and asked how it felt.

He said, "Okay, Mom, it was just really cold."

I told him that Ryan loved him so much and appeared to be checking up on him. I let him know that I saw and heard Ryan too and that I was thankful he told me. I didn't have that open experience with my parents as a child, so it helped me learn to listen and support my own.

The Mediumship continued with Ryan for another two months, and while that happened, I was coming to terms with letting go of my business. I ran a home daycare program and found it very difficult to remain present to my kids and the others. It felt unfair to the children in my care, so I gave notice and closed my business.

The week drawing near the funeral, I was at my parents' scrolling messages from friends and family members on social media; I got a call from HR at the school board that said Ryan appointed me as his beneficiary. I was frozen and shocked. Receiving that was very emotional; I almost didn't feel worthy of accepting it. Why me?

Then my dad helped me; he told me Ryan informed him when he signed his paperwork after getting full-time at the school board as a custodian. He said, "I made Ashley my beneficiary for life insurance," and they both agreed that was a thoughtful thing to do, as he didn't have his own kids or family yet.

So often, we say, "THANK YOU, RYAN" for the many opportunities and blessings we've had in the last six years thanks to him.

I was able to take time for myself and support the family and my brother through his transition due to his generous decision.

In the years to come, I was able to be there for my kids in a way that may not have been possible without his help. I also acknowledge the generous support from my community of friends who showed up for our family in tremendous ways.

Ryan's role as an uncle was filled tenfold and brought honor to his life, which meant so much to my dad.

Ryan's spirit stuck around a while; he rode along with me while I facilitated a group meditation for six weeks after closing my daycare. He took part in making that memorable by offering ideas when I would meditate in the beautiful cemetery before arriving. I would meet him at a large maple tree at the back end of the cemetery, with a big open field beside me. Often the sunset would inspire and ground me before arriving for the group.

Ryan would hang out with me while I waited for the school bus to pick up my oldest son. He would arrive when my parents and I had a heart-to-heart talk. We would be gathered on the living room couches and Ryan would add his side or part in understanding the bigger picture.

At first this felt very vulnerable and scary for me to open to, but once my parents began opening to his communication and made healing connections for themselves it got easier.

I felt surprised by Ryan's contact, because I never knew when or how he would show up. Sometimes I saw him sitting on the couch or standing in the kitchen, while other times I heard his voice in my mind or felt his energy close but didn't see anything.

To explain how I experienced it, let's say you close your eyes and imagine an ice cream cone. You focus on the details, and it appears real in your mind. I saw spirits like that growing up, my two eyes could be open, but I would see Spirits or energy hovering or coming out of places with my mind's eye, the one we imagine with.

The second way to experience is if I put an ice cream cone on the counter and you walked by quickly, you would see it with your two eyes. I had many occasions as a teen and in my twenties where I saw with my two eyes translucent waves of color, full-bodied energy or physical imprints that showed something moving around me.

After many of those I decided I didn't want that experience because in a way that made my brain and body react bigger compared to when my mind's eye experienced it. When it felt less intense the fear wasn't as strong and I was able to feel safe in my body while exploring the energy. With the help of spiritual teachers, I learned that I get to decide how I want to be contacted, how often and if I want to at all. That was an empowering moment that changed my perspective, interactions and confidence.

Since the contact with Ryan, I was open to seeing him both with my two eyes and my mind's eye because he was my brother.

One night I arrived at my parent's house to give my mom Reiki with Erin.

I arrived earlier and sat in the truck for a while. Ryan's Spirit popped in shortly after me, but this time he was behind me, not beside me on the passenger side. I sensed seriousness from him; he knew why I had come; yet I felt humanness in his feelings. He came close to my back and asked me if I could do him a favor. I felt tension and caution riding within me as I listened further.

He asked if I would give him the experience of being in the garage one last time. The garage was his refuge, along with my dad, he called it "The Man Cave."

It was next to the house beside the back yard and had a big garage door and two patio doors out back. This place was where he would hide, nap, think, process, party, enjoy and contemplate worries. Ryan was in there late the night before he left for the cottage with Monica. He had honest words with our mother about his internal struggles. He wanted the trip to be just right for her and felt a lot of pressure to organize all the plans.

My mom was concerned for him, and he reassured her that night, that things were getting better and that he needed to ease his anxiety with plant medicine sometimes.

After his request, I asked him to give me a moment, as this is not something I would ever do, but it was my brother, so I gave it a chance.

I had built trust within myself for quite some time, but it was still a daily practice to ask my higher self before deciding on anything. To do that, I found my feet, centered myself and asked a question then waited to hear a clear yes or no in my mind. Other times I surrendered to my body as if it was a pendulum and let it move forward for yes or back for no.

Super cool! Feels great when I listen and move forward with clarity. In the truck that night, I checked in with my higher self whether this was safe or smart to do.

I felt no resistance; I felt a faint push forward and decided aloud, "Okay Ryan, let's try this." I asked him, "What's next?"

He said, "Relax and wait."

My hands were on the steering wheel, parked in the driveway, darkness surrounded the truck, and streetlights lit up behind me. I felt a soft opening in the middle of my back, a light flow of energy slip through as if a zipper opened, allowing in a gust of wind and then closed behind it. Suddenly, I became aware of my hands like it wasn't my awareness. It was both of us, which felt unique viscerally. Ryan's Spirit was experiencing my hands on the steering wheel as if he remembered that feeling. I saw my hands through both our lenses. I told him how weird it felt, but it was okay. "Now what?" I asked.

He requested that I go into the garage when I was ready. I remember slowly walking there very aware of my surroundings; I remember sitting down on a chair in the dark of the garage and feeling sad yet comforted. I stayed there for a while, allowing him space to be present through me. I didn't have many human thoughts at all; I felt feelings in my body and a deepened presence of the space. After leaving in the shocking way he did, I can only imagine how this must have felt to have another moment of experiencing an earthly space he knew so well.

I took a glimpse of my phone to check the time. My mom had been ready for Reiki, so I let him know the time was up, and in another moment, Ryan slipped out the same way he came in and thanked me for permission to do that.

I was in awe, yet again, that this happened and went inside to tell my mom.

Erin arrived shortly after, and we set up the small computer room on the upper floor where the Reiki table was set up. We both offered Reiki to my mom. Ryan came in, standing near her head; my mom later shared after the session how she felt another pair of hands on her besides Erin's and mine. What a gift that he joined us!

Around this time, I started to experience mental burnout symptoms. I was in and out of awareness throughout the day. I reacted irrationally and felt a growing amount of stress. I would disassociate with my kids, and often feeling tired but kept holding on to Ryan.

I had survived two burnouts before, through the stress of working in youth residential care settings, living with my sensitivities and being a recovering co-dependent. It can be easy for me to get fatigued, spent, and challenged in coping with anxiety and the demands of life as an exceptional human.

Ryan was getting so involved in helping and enjoying the process. I didn't want to let go of him. He got himself into other communications and began helping other lost Spirits, which I later pieced together with Ryan and a friend. A week later, I could not see him or sense his presence. I was confused as it was so effortless up until then. I could hear him in faint ways, but he felt so far away, comparable to being in a large deep tunnel that I couldn't see.

I wondered if he was beginning to cross over or shift into the "next place."

There was a distressing feeling to his energy, he felt so far away and confused; he questioned how he got there or where he was. At this point, I reached out to some teachers of mine for some advice, who suggested I take some time to ground myself and try to set the intention of reaching out to him.

One evening intuitively prompted, I grounded myself while sitting on my bed.

I anchored my intention to reach his energy to help guide him back. It felt like echolocation that dolphins use to communicate. On the edge of my bed, I continued to call his name and sent with my mind's eye, what felt like mind lines out to where he was. I kept speaking to him within my mind and sent out my love, and he told me he could hear me. He asked that I continue to call to him; he followed my calls back to where I was. To this day, I still don't understand what I did, but he was back in my home, and I became more honest about how tired I was becoming.

My life was asking me to come back too. My husband and I went through a lot with our kids, roles, and relationship, so we began seeing a family counselor, who helped us put things into perspective. Brandon continued to go to therapy on his own, which was a massive shift for him personally, and to this day, we continue to benefit from his courage to get his own support, along with joint help too. It's the support that continued to expand within our family, our relationships and accountability to us.

I began bereavement counseling through Durham Hospice as my burnout progressed. Durham Hospice offered a grief support partner; I was given the opportunity to meet different volunteers; choose which one felt best.

After my first meeting with the coordinator, she later called to tell me the volunteer was named Grace; I felt my body tingle.

I chuckled and told her, "Oh, she's the one," before even meeting her. My intuition was spot on. We met a week later in the office building. Grace had lost a brother, husband, and mother.

She was a very spiritual woman, and she was such a massive part of my healing. We talked and processed together each week for an hour, a whole nine weeks. Each visit I shared what was showing up in my grief. She helped guide my healing by listening and sharing her experiences too, so I didn't feel so alone. I'm so grateful for Grace, she was like an angel.

During that time, I also reached out to an old guide and friend and signed up for four weeks of spiritual coaching, which helped me place my experiences, guide me through what was transforming within me, and helped me get back to my reality.

Unpacking the fears of Mediumship with Ryan's loss had generational layers. I had been silent about it for so long, then suddenly dropped in the middle of it with people who are not usually open or interested. It was not a topic that my dad enjoyed talking about which contributed to the silence as a kid, but he had good reason.

My mom just didn't believe that was possible.

I've learned that practice, patience, trust, and validation are part of crafting the art of intuitively receiving and offering. I had to explore this on my own outside of my family. I had incredible teachers over the last ten years that have helped me navigate these gifts and I honor and thank them greatly; you've all supported my growth. I healed the abandoned parts of myself that resulted in not understanding what was happening to me and met others like me.

Many experiences made up my willingness to explore this channel of communication with Ryan. I just never imagined being on this side holding space for Ryan in this way. There wasn't too much I wouldn't do for him, but I also got clear with support that something had to give, or I was heading into a third burnout.

I was intuitively guided towards a man named Steve, which began the transition phase. In the same way I help the young boy spirit, it was time to help Ryan move on.

8: It's Time to Leave

Friends and family gathered at my aunt Yvette's house, approximately two weeks after Ryan died. Her friends were telling stories about Ryan. Steve arrived at the crowded dining room and heard of Ryan's passing. He reacted with shock and asked to see a picture of him. Lo and behold, there was Ryan, the young man he had just met days ago. Steve, with his bright eyes and a loud, passionate voice, said, "No flipping way; I just met this guy the other day. He was so bright; his energy was so strong it was unreal."

My mother was taken aback by Steve's description, which was the beginning of our journey with Steve. He has been a friend to my aunt and uncle for over thirty years, and this connection remind me that the universe sure does work in mysterious ways, we just need to pay attention. The right people come into your life for reasons you are ready for but sometimes aren't fully conscious of yet. Answers and wisdom come with time and experience, thus making them conscious.

This man could keep up with my wild spiritual adventures, intuitive sight, and meditative experiences. He became an inspiring light that guided me, and I felt less alone when supporting Ryan's Spirit as it had become heavy. I was so used to feeling like an oddball, misunderstood or alone on my wild, expansive island. Steve anchored in the shine with me.

I thank and honor him for that.

My mom, aunt, and I agreed to meet him in person about a month and a half later and I began sharing personal experiences with my brother. Ryan guided me to give him a selenite wand, which appeared like an icy white crystal. As the evening went on, my mother and aunt tried to keep up with our discussion topics but at times felt a bit scattered. Then Steve redirected the attention to Ryan towards the end of the night.

Steve said, "Ryan isn't going to like this very much, but it needs to be said. It's time that he moves on and go towards the light." I could instantly feel Ryan's energy shift and pull back, but we continued to discuss further.

"I know he's enjoying himself and being in the middle of all this action helping others, but his purpose is to continue on the other side," Steve finished.

I acknowledged the truth, and it was relieving for me to hear it. Another burnout began for me already but I assured Ryan that we would talk about it; we finished our conversation and I left with a new mission.

On the ride home to my house, Ryan was in the truck, and I encouraged him to give it a try. I said, "I can hear and see you, so why would it be any different on the other side?" I suggested that he visit our dad, who was at our cottage. My dad had dreams of Ryan but really wanted a chance to connect with him in similar ways that I did. Just like that, Ryan left, and I had one heavy heart to hold but knew the time was right. I went to sleep not feeling him and prayed that both my father and brother could make a connection like the one I experienced—*Time to let go some more, Ashley*, I told myself.

Up until this point, my parents had experienced some connections with Ryan near bedtime upon falling asleep, and my dad's second time was shortly after Ryan died. He felt a cold touch on his ankle; after opening his eyes, he saw no one standing there. The third time was a light push moving his ankle off his other leg at the cottage. When Ryan was alive and needed to wake my dad from naps, that was his method of waking him, a touch or nudge on his ankle.

My mom began seeing wisps of bright white light swirling above her bed at night that would feel just like him. She experienced this for many months. After my mom, it began to happen similarly for my dad. He saw blue lights and swirls when he was at the cottage in bed. He lifted his hand and touched what he saw, and it surrounded his arm and felt tingly.

It was so special for them to receive the contact.

The morning after Steve's conversation, I went about my routine as usual; some water and oatmeal. I took a seat at the desktop computer in our basement; it felt a bit dark and damp. As the screen lit up, I felt the pull and slow energy of Ryan behind me. It appeared like his head was hanging low, and I wondered what happened up north.

There wasn't much to exchange; Ryan failed to make contact with our dad, like he hoped. He felt down but knew it was time to go. So, I asked if there was anything that I could do for him.

He asked, *Can you write for me?* I said, "Of course."

I began typing letters as he shared them. The request was for my Aunt Yvette, Uncle Paul, and Dad. As I re-read the last one aloud while sitting in the computer chair, I spontaneously felt energy pull upwards without knowing or trying. The only way to describe it was as if a tunnel or tornado spun up from the top of my head and reached the roof rooting into the base of my spine. It moved towards the ceiling, and I saw a motorbike wheel pull into the space above my head. Ryan was rising through the tunnel as I realized what was starting to take place.

It was his ride to heaven.

When Ryan was alive, we lost our cousin Steven to a motorcycle accident in Ajax, Ontario. He was my Aunt Anita's son on my dad's side. Steven also sustained a serious head injury, which took his life. As Ryan approached the motorcycle above me, he jumped on the back with Steven, and off the two of them went. I was in awe and disbelief. They left, the tunnel above me disappeared and I knew it was his time.

Right away I texted my close friends, family, and Steve, and asked everyone to light a candle and visualize Ryan moving towards the light. The next few days were quiet, and it was days away from Halloween. For anyone interested, Halloween finds its roots in the Ancient Celtic Fire Festival known as Samhain.

Samhain marked the end of the lighter half of the year, or growing months, and the beginning of the darker half—an inward time, winter. It was also a time where the boundary between this world and the other world was fluid and thinnest, meaning spirits could pass through. Samhain was a time where families venerated, honored and celebrated their ancestors, and those recently passed. I found this to be an exciting time for Ryan to make his passage.

While writing this chapter, five years later, it happens to be a couple of days after Samhain, which I found super cool and synchronistic.

After Ryan left with Steven, I gathered close friends and their children the night of Samhain/Halloween, and we built a fire in our backyard. Surrounded by beautiful young hearts, we sent light and prayers Ryan's way, explaining how his soul was making passage to heaven/the other side to the kids. I will never forget how touched I felt at that moment, the kids made it so special.

I would be lying if I said I was relieved. It had been an exciting adventure. The spontaneous exchanges, the deep sharing with family, keeping the close connection alive with Ryan had felt so good. After he left, it became a waiting game. I was doubtful. Was it going well for him? Where was he now? Would I hear from him? All these questions flooded my mind as I waited.

Family members would check in with me to see if I heard or sensed anything. I was honest; I didn't. We all felt decreased activity; a new loss to process but grateful for his moving on. We began going about our lives again.

Nothing prepared me for the stages of grief; I believe it's something each person experiences in their own unique way. This felt like a third grief, second to the funeral.

Steve, Mom, and I continued to gather for tea and conversations, which stretched for months. It was comforting to keep the flow going with someone who had communications with Ryan. It took a while for Ryan to make a connection again; it was months later that the faint sound of his voice returned.

I experienced him differently after he crossed over. I no longer saw his Spirit body in the room, I saw him in many light tones hovering above me or near the ceiling. He returned with the same humor and big love, maybe even a bit bigger. There was a space or distance between us that I didn't feel before, but I sustained clear communication, that came through my mind or when I felt his light and presence. He was so bright, and I often saw him in many colors of blue and white light. His messages began encouraging me to listen with my whole heart, trust in myself, and work together with him. I wasn't sure what that meant at the time, but I was gearing up to give it a try.

Steve had opened to Ryan and helped us both through that challenge of letting go. When Ryan's consciousness returned; he tuned in with Steve to ask a favor one day at work in his truck. Steve had never been asked a task like this before by a Spirit; it was an involved commitment. With consideration, he agreed.

Since that day, morning, and evening, the two of them unite in a meditative state of light, and both send healing light to this planet. There is much more those two have explored together that Steve and I continue to gather and talk about but that will be enough for this book.

Ryan began showing up when it mattered for me in times of struggle; he became a guiding light and helpful inner voice I received dialogue back and forth with. His messages always seemed to move my heart in the right direction when I needed it.

Now so many years later, I look back and see how joining up together with him genuinely changed my life on the inside. I have grown to love and trust myself in ways I struggled with before. This helped me whole-heartedly open fully to my intuitive Reiki practice and business. I cultivated new relationships with my parents and continued to find courage to express myself honestly. My boys had a chance to express themselves through their spiritual encounters in a way I didn't growing up; this brought so much healing to us all.

There was another significant death that happened between the communications and healing of our family that's important to share. This loss impacted our family and became another opportunity to delve deeper into layers of inner healing.

9: Not Another Son

Ryan was very anxious and guarded with his deep feelings and hid his relationship with Monica from most of us, perhaps because he didn't trust the questions we would ask or feared judgment or embarrassment; I will never know. What I do know is that he didn't hide her from our oldest half-brother Paul.

Ryan would discreetly find ways to make others feel important, chosen, and cared for, while in silent struggle himself. In his mid-twenties he was diagnosed with generalized anxiety and a social phobia. The anxiety appeared in many areas of his life, with extreme self-critical fears around social situations. He had heightened empathy, and expressed deep concern for others' feelings or needs, while struggling to feel worthy enough to meet or support his own needs. He had been through so much himself, yet he went out of his way for those to whom he felt drawn.

One day, Ryan brought Monica over to Paul's home in Keswick to meet his family as a couple for the first time. That meeting would have meant the world to Paul. He was a family man through and through. He showed up for people in his life and gave the clothes off his back for those in need.

Paul had expressed to his wife that he felt like an outsider in our family, as he had different choices and experiences growing up. He lived with us much later into his teens and only for a short while until he moved out on his own. Paul sometimes felt different from the three of us, but it was far from true. We loved him the same, but when I told Ryan about this, Ryan wanted Paul to feel important and included.

I'm telling you about Paul because similar things lined up for him before he died; yes, another brother left us. Similarly, it was an accidental death; the car accident left him with a severe brain injury from which he would never be the same. Months leading up, things in his life began to line up as he struggled internally like Ryan. Ongoing home renovations were almost complete; as his wife told me, he had been working on replacing many parts of his home for the last fifteen years.

It was one of his passions, along withstanding up for his men at work as a foreman and safety rep for scaffolding, which he had been in for forty years. Paul always had a project going, whether his own or helping family or friends.

A toxic work dispute that resulted in threats from a co-worker got resolved in Paul's favor just months before the accident. His birth-daughter Carly got married, and we all enjoyed the celebration together as family days before the accident occurred. On the day of, he was on the road home to see the newly finished kitchen, but he never made it.

His accident was at the end of day rush hour on a large highway; that evening I had been at the cottage with my youngest child and parents. The fireplace was warm and comforting, a beautiful color of orange and yellow. After bedtime routine, we had just finished some evening shares, and my mom's phone rang.

It was Laura, Paul's wife, and she was breathing heavily and could hardly talk. We all listened anxiously through silent moments. My mom encouraged her to take a breath and take her time.

"It's Paul," she said.

My heart sank, which I am sure anyone who got one of those calls before would know.

I became highly aware of my dad's reaction and emotions within my body; I witnessed him put his head down into his hands and say, "Dear God, not another son."

We listened further, and she told us, "Paul's been taken to the hospital; there was an accident." That's all she knew. Police were at her door, and we heard the dog barking in a panic through the phone.

My parents agreed to drive to Sunnybrook Hospital and told her they would see her soon.

Laura informed them that her sister-in-law would take her, and the phone call ended.

My dad took refuge in his room while getting ready to go. My mom and I tried to develop optimistic views of what could have happened. The heaviness ran deep, and they got ready quickly; the hospital was hours away.

I had to stay behind; my child was asleep, and I decided all I could do was pray and send Reiki healing his way. The room was dark and quiet after they left. I called a couple of friends to share the news and process my feelings about what had just happened. Then I became reticent. Could I connect with him? Was it possible to read into his energy and send light that would help? I was confident of one thing: the power of prayer and light. So that's what I did.

I received texts informing me he was in the ICU and had lost a lot of blood. The hospital tried all they could to help him. He had gone through bags and bags of donated blood to save his life. The waiting room filled up with his friends and family members anxiously ready to hear any news. Yet we kept hearing he had too many injuries, and transfusions were not successful.

As I tuned in energetically to his Spirit from the cottage, I intuitively sensed an impact to the right side of his head and internal damage on the left. I felt his Spirit coming in and out of staying or going.

I sent light anyways, in complete surrender. Later when I did see his body, the right side of his face and head was ballooned.

My parents had the second-longest drive of their life, apart from Ryan's hospital drive. Paul's mother was on her way too with my brother Peter and many others.

The next morning, I ate breakfast with my son and took space outside, praying for Paul's recovery. While sitting on the same protruding rock that I sang on the evening of Ryan's death,

I witnessed Paul's Spirit in a holographic white tone above my head in the sky. I asked him, "What will draw you back to your body and life here?" I was pleading that he focus on staying in his body. I was taken aback but not surprised that the answer was making love to his wife; then quickly vanished from view and contact.

Into the late morning, I packed up to leave and decided to have my husband meet me and pick up our son. I was anxious to drive to the hospital. When I arrived, everyone there took me by surprise. They took up a whole section of the waiting room. I went right to Laura, hugged her, and asked if I could offer her some Reiki. Sometimes words are just too hard, so I felt most helpful with my silent healing hands.

Halfway through offering Reiki, there he was. I saw and sensed Paul's Spirit body pass through the doorway of the ICU; he came out. Through my mind's eye, I saw his hair, the structure of his body in a light grey yet clear and transparent tone. His chubby fingers rose as he approached me, pointing at Laura. I heard him say, *My wife, my wife, my wife.*

He finished with, *I will be back.*

There was a railing I was standing beside, overlooking another waiting room below. The building wall was tall; many windows reached the ceiling halfway up. Then into my vision came Ryan's Spirit, clear and transparent through one of the tallest windows. He hovered above the ICU floor. I sensed a pull or draw towards him, and I watched Paul's Spirit rise to join Ryan's; and they left out the window together.

When these encounters happen to me, it often feels strange because I'm alone in the experience. It's not like, "Did everyone just see that?" Well, no! I quietly told Laura what I saw and what he said. She began crying and affirmed that would be him.

My dad approached, asking if I wanted to go into the ICU and see him together. I agreed.

Anyone who has been in there knows the multiple beeping sounds, busy nurses moving around quickly, doctors reviewing screens and scared humans waiting for help.

We came to Paul's bed, and it was like looking at an empty body suit; I felt no spirit or life essence within it. It became uncomfortable with the potency of him leaving, and told my dad I didn't feel him in there; we both agreed and returned to the waiting room.

That evening, after a brain scan, they found out that Paul's brain injuries were irreparable and he would never want to return to life unable to be himself. So, with the power of family love, together we watched the unplugging and said goodbye.

The vital message from that experience for me is that we indeed are never alone, even on the other side. There are so many things as humans we can't comprehend or explain; we may never have enough studies or proof. I began to open my heart to the world of Spirit and energy. Especially when it came to my family, my blood or someone very dear to me. It taught me that Spirit is mysterious and takes a life of its own and truly interacts with me in miraculous ways. It's something that can be felt individually with the heart, for me brought so much good change within myself.

Profound interactions, messages, and experiences became part of my new reality. It's not for everyone, and that's okay. I witnessed people get drawn together through their pain and began evaluating their life and asked questions they weren't aware of before; perhaps made time to ponder.

I observed both through Ryan and Paul; their lives became a jigsaw puzzle. Through the loss, we pieced parts of their lives together after they died; it was intriguing because talking about the struggles while they were here didn't happen openly. It may have been too hard, shame-filled, self-preservation, maybe embarrassing, or perhaps they were just not ready or wanting.

But death had a way of stripping away all those layers and protections we hid behind.

The vulnerability of loss, pain, and mending the heart became more vital to continue here.

We healed together by talking about the hard stuff and took our time with each other and ourselves, respecting our differences in processing grief but gentle nudges to continue moving forward.

I believe shame has silenced so much of humanity, when we are conditioned for so long to hide the realness, the struggle, to be "good enough" or "seen/accepted" by others.

I accept that it's time to honor both sides of being human; easier said than done. The discomfort and the pleasure are forces that I am learning to dance with and accept as part of being here. What has made it possible to practice communication and have courage to be real and honor the feelings in between, was community of like minds and compassionate friends. I am often taken back in awe when I am open and real with others, it gives them permission to do the same. When I leave that interaction, I have a deep sense that something great happened to us both. I hope we can all find more opportunities to share with others in heart-centered ways to find the good together, because it ripples change. Change we truly wish to see in this world right now.

At Paul's funeral, a man approached my father to tell him, "Your son saved my life." Years before, that man had a girlfriend with a baby on the way while heading down a dangerous road with drugs. When Paul heard of this, he went directly to this worker and had an honest talk with him. Paul coached him to take his baby and family seriously, that their workplace had programs to get clean, and he was there to help him if he needed. The man took the advice, got clean, returned to work, and told my dad he was happy with a baby girl, all thanks to Paul. This news moved my dad to tears, I am sure

Paul felt great about his part and we were so grateful for that man's vulnerable share.

Each person grieves differently, but somehow, we connect to what's important and begin living differently without realizing it. The courage to be real with others is one of our greatest opportunities. I'm not saying it's easy or we all need to jump on this wagon of share my life story with everyone. Perhaps a small doable step towards honesty with self is a start, then permission to let someone, of your choice, hear and see you a little more. Then, bit by bit, it grows and people around you get inspired and new connections get made that bring new spirit into your life.

So many years later, I can confidently say we are all changed people, with learned acceptance, humility, willingness, and closeness. I often imagine my brothers back in our lives. It feels like a joyful fantasy, but I've come to accept the depth of their love in this new way.

I wonder if they see their purpose, and how much healing came from who they were while they were here. I believe so. Let grief move you towards those who are still here and pray for the patience to heal, allowing that to ripple out into your life.

10: Fundamental Ruptures and Growth

For as long as I can remember, I gave myself to others in order to cultivate safety and worth.

Due to my sensitive nature, I believe I did this to avoid getting uncomfortable or hurt in situations. If I just took care of things around me or avoided them altogether, I could manage how painful things became or control the outcome to ensure my safety. I identify today as a recovering co-dependent. In my own words healing from co-dependency means finding the balance between giving and receiving and awareness of the source from which I'm giving.

Is it joy or obligation? Is it a desperate need to be chosen or a grounded choice with intent and clarity? Am I controlling and fixating for safety or flowing and fueling myself naturally when helping others? Instead of focusing so much on what others need, I've learned to consider my own needs, make them a priority and move towards serving second. When I override my boundaries, I can get upset with others and myself or get defensive trying to prove why I am in need.

While navigating many confusing emotional experiences growing up, naïve at times, I'd get caught in many opposing opinions or energy of others. Even though I felt in my heart that I was doing right by my choices, being who I was, or standing up for others, I began second-guessing the validity of my inner guidance system. I started to seek out others' approval, opinions, or ideas to formulate my own decisions; I'd wait to be affirmed by a boss, teacher, parent, friend, or authority figure before feeling confident in my thoughts and decisions. I sought external sources to ground into so that I felt confident to guide myself.

In turn, I was giving my power away. To differentiate, receiving guidance and returning to my own-grounded sense of self to decide, to me is health. I had become dependent upon others to decide, feel confident and navigate life altogether.

Wild as a young girl, you wouldn't see me sitting reading a book. I was always moving, doing, thinking, or processing. I was not very focused in school; I talked a lot and struggled academically and socially with peers. Misunderstanding this at the time, while also being highly empathic and feeling the world through my body created a heightened "on guard" sense that often distracted me a lot of the time. I worked hard academically, and my parents paid for extra support so I could access my skills. I didn't have many friends and was a target for being picked on about many different things, which hurt me and created core insecurities.

I caught myself in trouble trying to be a tough girl as I grew up, picking fights with boys or trying to show how strong I was in sports. It became part of my habitual behavior to prove myself, my worth and value. I resented people that brought it out of me more. The small group of friends I did have were close ones that I felt I could be myself with; for that, I am grateful.

When young, I walked the woods alone at my cottage or in Nova Scotia. I felt big in an even bigger world yet never felt alone or afraid. The trees felt like protectors, the ground was my comfort, and the unknown was an adventure. I felt free. Free to imagine, free to wander, free to create and build. The silence, a friend back then but I was far from silent.

My inner voice was filled with ideas, and imagination as a child. I loved running around pretending to be on horseback, I felt alive, like inside of me was the Spirit of the horse. To this day, I continue to have dreams of horses as a reminder to hold true to my wild side, the part of me that desires freedom and Spirit to be expressed.

Later in adolescence, the inner voice became quite the inner critic, people pleaser, joker and anxious over thinker, that I still redirect today.

Nature had and continues to gift me a platform from which to be and explore. The slow beauty offers my body and system to let down, breathe deeper and ponder what is important inside myself. Nature has an intelligence that can connect me to the unseen and the spirit within.

Mother Earth deserves all our attention to keep this connection alive, healthy and in balance because without her we are gone and the growth of imbalance will continue to manifest within us as disease, sickness, pain and suffering.

This human journey wraps up into so many moments, not just with me but many others. Being human, for me is a chance to grow my soul. Other souls give me the opportunity to play out my lessons so I can get clearer about whom I am and what I want to express and create here. A vital awareness that became clear as I moved through grief and allowed myself to let go is that ego plays a massive part in my human experience. Learning when it works with or against me has become vital in my inner peace.

As time went on, I grew up and became inspired to help others and share my bright side with many people. I believed life was good, with many parts being a privilege and joy.

I went to college and trained to support children and youth at risk, chose customer service jobs; loved interacting with people of all ages. I navigated many relationships with males that showed me how I continued to put others' needs before my own.

I met Brandon when I was sixteen years old. We dated for three years. He was too kind and treated me well; I struggled to appreciate that in a way he deserved. It's as if I was being guided into struggle to learn more about myself. I broke up with him in a very kind and meaningful way; I halted our relationship but kept that love open for possibility at another time. After six years apart and seeing other people, learning lots of hard lessons, I reunited with him, open to receiving his kind loyal heart and we created our family.

That's when I began exploring my inner world and sought counseling, as this relationship with him was one of mutual respect and safety. I surprised myself getting to know my patterns, behaviors, and inner landscape. I naturally helped others and was happy doing it, meanwhile, hiding all the ruptured, unregulated parts of myself behind helping and gaining self-worth outside myself. There was a fundamental rupture within me that began when I was five, and it was time to unfold and heal since it dictated my relationships, decisions, and connection with myself.

Ryan's death offered a chance for more of these old beliefs to surface as I genuinely listened to my inner being in a deeper way after he left. The grief put my needs at the forefront within my own family, and there was space to share my sensitivities, Mediumship with Ryan and seek further guidance. I often gave Ryan a lot of credit, as he was the catalyst or soul agent responsible for so much of my growth. I've slowly learned to acknowledge my efforts, Ryan guided me back to myself, but I chose to listen and do the work, and encouraged others to join me.

One of my most treasured gifts is my Empathic intuition. However, it's been part of my long streak of burnouts too. I have felt shame, guilt, and insecurity about it for many years. Especially when it kept me from doing things, I knew I could do well. Today, the challenges empower me to listen more closely, choose and advocate for my needs and learn to love myself through my exceptionalities.

When Ryan left, it transformed the way we connected; we were close as children, but this brought us closer, and I got a chance to build something even more substantial between us. Being human can be daunting sometimes, with thoughts and emotions driving so many interactions and experiences. With me here on this side and him on the other, it offered a new chance to meet him and myself in a way that wasn't possible while he was here.

Being at the edge of burnout isn't fun for anyone, and I believe it happens more often than we realize. This progressive pressure that society has humans accustomed to living under, pushing past needs and boundaries; numbing what we are feeling to cope and get through. It takes a severe toll on people's mental, emotional and physical health. Some people thrive in that, which is excellent; we need them. In time even for them, it may catch up, reminding them of their humanness with health concerns or personal needs to address.

I speak for myself; I've had recurring challenges most of my life with stress, pain, injuries, and burnout being empathically sensitive. I've learned to nurture my gifts as an intuitive healer to be of service to help others, but at the same time, I need to balance my own needs with self-care, humor, and teamwork.

I believe sensitive compassionate humans tune into this world in their unique ways that create helpful points of view for the whole to consider. This awareness can help our planet and humanity. As I look around today, I see the need to bridge human compassion together again. No human is perfect; we were made by design that way. I believe we learn throughout our lives so we can remember who we are: a Spirit having a human experience. So, if we are all a Spirit, made from the same essence of life, can we begin to turn in with love versus out with fixated blame or shame? It takes each of us to do our part to re-create a new whole.

About a year after Ryan left, we began what I like to call "Coaching with Ryan." One day in March, he asked me to start a set of practices while I was journaling on my computer at the front window desk at home. I practiced slow deep breaths while imagining myself grounded into the earth and connected above to the sky, emptying all my thoughts to turn into my center. Then I practiced dropping my neutral energy into the bottom of my spine and visualized Ryan. At that time, I said his full name and date of birth: Ryan Anthony Vincent Tyms, born July 11, 1987. Then I waited.

The first time I tried, about five minutes later, there he was. I could hear his voice in my head. I began typing his response with (R:). I typed my questions or answers with (A:). This continued consistently from March 2018 until October 2021.

We communicated like this twice a week for the first year, but in the years that followed, I made space when I heard him say, *Make time for me*, or when I felt the need for support and guidance. He explained his reason for doing this was to help me fine-tune my abilities and get ready for what was next. Thinking back now, it was this book and the balance I practice being an Intuitive Reiki practitioner, mother, and wife. He said he would always meet me where I was and come through as a channel of love and clarity. Looking back now, that's exactly what it offered.

At the beginning I asked him how I could keep from letting my ego get the best of these appointments. I feared I might get in the way.

He said, *Reach for the ground and sky, remain silent in your heart until you feel an easy flow of energy or words coming from me.* So that was my practice, and I did it consistently with him and within my Reiki sessions. Ryan encouraged me, pointed out where I was trying too hard, lifted me up, answered my questions, and challenged my humanness.

Being vulnerable with him became my safe place to be heard and loved no matter what.

In my experiences, sharing vulnerably sometimes felt unsafe, scary or anxious. I began counting on these coaching conversations and they helped me grow connections within myself. Through that grounded safety I grew on the inside which also expanded into my other relationships too. When it didn't feel good with someone in particular, I just chose someone that did. If there weren't other safe people, I would choose Ryan, a counselor or myself through journaling. I only shared a couple of Ryan's messages to family members a handful of times when it was relevant or inspired. I have learned whom I can trust with the tender parts of me and whom I experience different parts of myself with. I practice the act of discernment which has been a brilliant tool to access and will always be something I'm crafting and growing further in awareness.

One day I asked Ryan if he could describe where he was, he responded with, *It's like being in the middle of rainbow colors that aren't colors. They are real live beams of existence. It's like swimming in a pool of so much feel-good that you don't know where you end and begin. I love it here. It's freedom. I can see specks in the 'colors' that I can choose to help or not. I can go with what you would call your mind's eye, and I can access people or other existence and decide how to help. This is a simple way of trying to explain it.*

The colors he described reminded me of a Netflix special I watched. People who had near-death experiences explained how they died and returned; then telling of the great colors they saw or felt and how good it was to be there on the other side. People on the show described it as a warm home feeling, and when coming back, their life wasn't the same. At a meeting in the show, the people gathered had near-death experiences and all shared having a yearning to make things better on Earth once they came back. They expressed the want to return to where their death took them, and all had some form of struggle to relate to this life in the same way.

I related to that, since young I had an innate want to be in harmony with nature. As I grew older and visited many planes of existence through meditation or shamanic medicinal journeys, I too found returning to this place challenging and yearned to be part of making it so much better for us all and beyond.

Throughout our coaching, Ryan reminded me of things from when we were young; he would catch me when I was hard on myself. He used humor and encouraged ideas to keep me going. He told me to find him in the sky and open to messages that moved me. It could be a cloud shape, a sunset, a bird or the expanding night sky. One message I received was:

Anything is possible beyond your perception if you can open yourself and expand into the thought. Rest and heal. And so, it is.

When things got tough within relationships, Ryan would have a way of piecing together essential parts of the lesson, so I remembered my part. He would always tell me, *You were designed for this, Ashley,* and although some days I laughed or cried, I began believing it.

I would even get-tough love; he would tell me not to come to him for answers I already had inside of me. Ryan would say, *Shame is killing your life force and focus on beating it!*

He told me, *Dreamtime will always give you warnings and to trust them above all, even me.* My brother shared that ups and downs help us get clearer. He directed me to listen to my body, go to bed and trust that I would get through.

This coaching helped me cultivate confidence; it taught me to trust what was inside me and have faith in Spirit. Some things need explanations of the mind, and I honor that. Some things are felt with my heart and become a part of me, gifting me an experience that only I can truly understand. This experience with Ryan strengthened my inner landscape and intuition, which sustains and guides me in everything I do today. Some days it's clear and strong, while other days, my humanness is louder, and I take that as a signal to simplify, slow down and care for my needs. My spark of Spirit always comes back, and it gives this human physical core a consciousness and ability to experience and grow on earth.

Grief has many stages and yet offers something unique in each one; it's not only the loss of people in our lives. Sometimes grief shows up in re-evaluating or losing relationships. It can show up as injury or sickness, losing the ability to move, think, function in the same way, or believe in ourselves. It takes time; support and tools are components that all human beings deserve to have access to.

Emotions move through each of our bodies in unique ways, in turn, guiding us to our own. From there, we can create new opportunities that simply weren't possible otherwise.

One way I experienced humble new beginnings was through singing. I used it to feel my connection to God; harmonizing sound made me feel alive and still does. It provided me relief from tension and helped me connect to a higher source. Nikola Tesla stated powerfully: =, "If you want to find the secrets of the universe, think in terms of energy, frequency and vibration."

Harmonizing sounds and high vibrational music can lift my energy into a higher frequency. Years ago, especially sung in nature, I overused my voice. I had lost my ability to sing like I used to after years of daycare settings, raising my kids and singing through grief. A tremendous change was needed to heal my throat and I was faced with a humbling choice. Push past my needs or put yourself in priority and accept the results of past choices.

In hindsight, I've learned through loss of my voice that I took it for granted. I didn't listen to my body. Inside me is a divine intelligence that waited every day to see if I would hear or choose to listen to her. Grief was my gateway to coming home to myself, listening to the needs of my body and it continues still.

While being human, duality exists; within that duality are two sides. Opposing beliefs, good and bad, enjoyable and displeasing or wrong and right. Each side creates waves to discover balance. Will we ever be wholly balanced and have everything figured out? Probably not, but I will continue to ride the waves with the intention of balance at my core. It's in the bouncing, disagreeing, questioning, and feeling that we co-create together with duality.

I think a clearer understanding of the world and depths that make up our human psyche comes alive through struggle, joy, resistance, and acceptance. This was my second humble beginning after loss; that so much energy gets used up trying to be right and totally understood by others. I've learned to put that energy into me, so I understand myself. I learned that listening to others is more about giving them space to be heard and expressed and let the duality guide me into clarity for myself. Sometimes it's a shared experience or being with like minds, which feels affirming and aligned. I also enjoy a healthy debate or sharing of differences.

What's changed for me is that I need not prove others wrong; I choose to come to an understanding of each other and set peaceful goals so we can move through our differences.

Still an ongoing practice!

It was my thirty-sixth year around the sun after my brother Paul died. Ryan moved us through a heartrending level of pain and love, while Paul reminded us with his love that nothing was ever certain to stay the same but to hold close to those we love.

When Ryan died, he continued making an impact on us through our channeling. To this day, he continues evolving and expanding with bright light helping in many ways where he is now. He feels light years away, yet his speck of light can still penetrate my heart every once in a while most of his humanness that I remember, is gone.

Dark and light will continue to be in constant motion with each other. I choose to embrace them both and learn to experience them with an open mind and compassionate heart. Like Ryan, we continue to grow into the best versions of ourselves and that choice is there to make each day. I continue to realize who I am, reinvent it with all that I learn and remember the source of all creation lives within everyone.

I'm learning to accept the things I am unable to change and focus on what I can. I can see that we innately all want to belong, feel connected to something, and invest in a purpose. To embody this, I am cultivating self-compassion, and I lend that out to others as much as I humanly can. The process of embodying self-love has many layers and stages, as it becomes who I am, I no longer need to try so hard. The source of being is coming from within me and outward to the world.

Throughout this story, I spoke of childhood past, loss, Mediumship and sensitivities. I'd like to close out with perspectives that came from courage to heal, showing up for one another and the possibilities of grief. Perhaps, it can offer you something to help you along your path.

11: We Can Heal

I want to wrap you all up in a big warm hug and thank you for making it this far through my story. I want to leave you with some positive perspectives from grief; its possibilities and where life may guide you with access to conscious choice and deeper awareness.

Chapter 11 felt important to me because Ryan's birthday was July 11. The number eleven is recognized to be a universal number and has a presence of a higher power that may help us along our way. My intention was to bring this story full circle back to the present-day, and the transformations that have come to our family since Ryan first left.

I didn't fully realize where this book was taking me throughout these last six years, even though I trusted something important was happening. My intention was to heal parts of myself and to bring about good to others. I now see the family healing on a larger scale, while being connected to my own in profound ways. I celebrate that as it continues!

This chapter took a while because I had to do some deep reflecting, prioritizing, letting go, and holding myself while exploring that potent middle layer of my inner core of root causes.

I chose after a family trip to Nova Scotia with my parents, aunt, and Nanny Agnes to evaluate my current crossroad. I could either continue pushing and hope not to burn out again or slow down, honor my boundaries, and invest in self-care for the purpose of my work.

Oftentimes I heard words or connections in my head for this book while doing mundane things. Like lying down for a five minute snuggle with my sons or while doing the dishes and looking out the window at the trees.

Certain mornings the warmth of my bed pulled me into its trap. I often wanted to relax back into comfort, not only when waking but in other parts of my life too. I rode a tricky edge of comfort and discomfort, as I learned that I could come to the edge of uncomfortable, persevere and then return to comfortable to bring ease to my system.

This book truly pushed my limits; forced me to sit with feelings that were uncomfortable.

To persevere for me isn't about sucking it up and pushing hard. It's about relying on inner or outer resources that help me move through the discomfort in a powerful conscious way.

I continue to titrate like this, giving my sensitive system a healthy balance between growth and rest. Some anxiety is good; it gets me to act, pushes me beyond what I knew possible. While too much anxiety can become a mental health struggle and can create symptoms of exhaustion, fear, worry or stop me from action. Knowing the difference and being able to differentiate in multiple situations has become a key resource. My higher self-led me through many strategies that pushed me out of those comfort levels writing this and helped me seek my own truth to share with you.

Get up now, it's time to write, I heard many early mornings.

My family had our own unique generational traumas and expectations that resulted in holding back truth and feelings to protect us. For some of us we masked through self-medicating, others pushed past boundaries to be accepted, while others rode on will and survival. Certain members went along with others to appease them out of fear of displeasing or being challenged. Many experienced guilt and shame, feeling responsible, wrong, blame, not being enough, too much, masking, being stuck, stubborn, wanting to be right or an overactive nervous system living in a state of hyperarousal or stress.

I acknowledge and honor every human's experience of generational ties and traumas. All you've endured to be here today and the courage to heal and create new. Each one of our stories matters and deserves to be heard.

There are many connections between my habits, relationships and circumstances. Exploring them became a mysterious path. Being highly Empathic and intuitive added a lens of enmeshment for me, where at times I struggled to know where I began and ended others in my life.

Empathy and intuition are two of my greatest gifts that offer incredible support, safe space and vision in my Reiki practice and warm presence in relationships. Many years of commitment, practice and training have gone into mastering my mind to bring me here today. I've practiced slowing down my mind, learning what triggers it, how it's connected to my body and feelings. Mastering the mind will always be a practice for me. I learned through different modalities to use intentional movement, strategic reflections, energetic alignment, diet, meditation, sleep, and breath to become aware, observe, and own myself. Through these practices, I am being accountable to the joy and suffering I experience.

My family's courage to patient and genuine with one another helped us navigate our way through loss. We began speaking truthfully, hearing one another, and owning our lives. The opportunity that grief gave us was to piece together what Ryan and Paul left behind and to talk about it out loud. I'm not going to lie; I cried a lot, I hurt, I wanted to give up, I hid, and I processed a lot with friends, professionals, and family members.

Somehow, we all wanted the same thing; we just had to become responsible for our own parts, expectations, habits, views, and judgements, and listen to one another. With time we each gained new awareness and I slowly learned how to redefine and ask for safe vulnerability. I chose to be a person in this family, to what we already knew, what we kept doing and begin learning how to do better.

I indirectly asked those I loved to follow me in whatever way worked for them. Yes, it took years to talk about hard topics without triggers. It also took many courageous attempts to speak up, ask for help, let myself be seen in tears or sadness and learn the balance between listening and sharing. I'm still learning to rest in my center, listen to my body and honor her. Grief offered us a platform of union because we had all loved and lost.

We all want to feel close and connected. Through the years of grief, we uncovered parts we masked to survive and that gave permission to be real. Our family aligned our intentions to become responsible for our parts, which we processed at our own pace.

Owning my parts recently led me to explore symptoms of my own ADHD, after an open conversation with a good friend. This diagnosis was not on my radar growing up or even in school studying Child & Youth Work. Was I in denial or just unaware? After listening to a couple great podcasts, I told my mom that I was relating to many features of ADHD. She then told me that Ryan was diagnosed with ADHD at thirteen years old. This was news to me; I was surprised that I wasn't informed.

I believe diagnosing can help to identify symptoms, and behaviors, that offer awareness, direction, and possible treatment ideas. Which can support healthy development and growth. One the flip side, diagnosis may have a downside, as it can be used as an excuse to avoid personal growth or change. Yet each person is responsible to explore unique aspects of themselves over time, at their own rate. I've had positive experiences professionally supporting young people with various conditions. Perhaps the years prior to my diagnosis helped me focus on my intuitive side and learn to respect my sensitivities.

With years supporting people's mental health, crisis work, professionally and personally, stress and loss took its toll on me. I began seeing the symptoms of ADHD, and how it connected with the anxiety, and stress I experienced for years.

Isolating myself as a young person and masking my struggles, resulted in misunderstanding myself. I learned these experiences gave me a chance to explore many parts of who I am, my purpose and re-invent myself. I crashed and burned but I also built and thrived. There's a natural ebb and flow supporting my soul housed in this human body. That soul is pure consciousness.

That part of me is light filled, ever expanding, and changing. I'm learning to let my Spirit be, in the moments that I can allow it and trust in the God source that I am.

After almost forty years I received a diagnosis of ADHD with adjustment features, and that was a process to receive. Not because I was surprised, but because the little girl inside of me came to the surface, had a voice, and was affirmed.

She was finally getting to hang up her mask, articulate her understandings and make connections about her past and struggles to be better understood. She and I both had to put into examples, words and revisit all the areas of life academically, relationally, loss, trauma, and stress to piece together that I often experience ADHD/anxiety both equally at times creating this vicious cycle.

Throughout the couple days after my appointment, it illuminated how often I pushed past my boundaries to fit in or please others. I compared myself to others who didn't have my challenges, thinking something must be wrong with me. Add seeing Spirits, feeling emotions of others as my own along with academic struggles no wonder self-esteem was an issue. This also pushed me to strive for success, to work hard to keep up and show others what I was made of. I discovered my strength.

Over time, trying so hard was one of the leading causes of burnout and the stress manifested into further anxiety and mental exhaustion. More recently, I've learned through Dr. Russell Barkely, who discusses ideas for parents and children with ADHD. That studies show that ADHD is more of an impairment of regulating emotions. That makes sense.

This is a fluctuating experience for me; I have spent ten years naturally healing my gut, learning the best food choices for my needs through elimination diet, supplement support, exercise, sleep, healing with Ryan's coaching, recovery counseling, and exploring root causes through energy healing and earth medicines, to now land here. Still practicing!

I had an opportunity to try medication for a short time to help me move from trying so hard, triggered by external stimulus and re-entering the vicious cycle. It did help get me back to a healthy baseline but unfortunately, due to my sensitivities, my body didn't do well; side effects were not ones I was going to live with. I am back trying new natural supplements, continuing my inner work, and crafting the discipline to keep the care in place that helps me.

Trying medication led me into further awareness and helped me set clear goals around how I want to feel in my body. I use regulation tools to balance, track my moods and woman cycles, document my tasks, and continue these practices today. I continue to learn further about ADHD and simplify my expectations, get a minimum of eight hours of sleep, eat enough protein and minerals, while offering compassion and patience towards my impaired executive functions. These help me to better cope with my exceptionalities.

I must credit the work of trusted coaching in my life over the last two years two incredible women, Tanya and Somer. Thank you. They both helped me widen my understanding and learn to listen to my body in a somatic way that helps me practice regulating my nervous system. It was a major resource to being able to process and hold myself powerfully through the diagnosing process. All my years of experience and study with mental health also helped me know the process of implementing, advocating and putting the right strategies into action.

I share this because it's important when doing any inner work, revisiting the past, exploring traumas, and getting to the root cause of mental or emotional challenges, to have a strong basis of support for the nervous system. Accumulating a toolbox for processing things within the body is essential for a healthy well-rounded experience. We all deserve to have support.

As I unpacked how I felt, and my upcoming changes, I faced some tender parts of myself while seeing the greater good and growth in my life. I named the shame I've carried for not fitting in like everyone else and comparing myself to find recognition. I felt sad that it took this long. I felt overwhelming fear about opening about it while also experiencing great clarity within myself that this was part of my life path the whole time.

For the longest time I felt hard-wired to explore the root causes of things, to get to the source of why someone's struggling and reflect on how it could become better. I questioned why Spirits were reaching out to me, why do things work a certain way, and can people and nature feel safe, happy and connected like I remember in my heart? I've always wanted peace here for everyone, just like John Lennon sang. I cry every time I listen to that song because my heart remembers, "YES, THAT!"

I don't share any of my experiences for pity or comparison, I share so that others may know they are not alone, I share to normalize. I want to move into further acceptance and loving compassion as an intuitive sensitive empath. I personally feel ADHD has qualities that challenge me but also make me wild, unique, creative, energetic and exceptional. When I created courage to publicly share this, honor the journey in my family, and stop hiding behind a wall of trying to appear like something I'm not, many symptoms began to loosen their grip. It's okay to be me. I continue to grow with acceptance as a resource through the hard times.

In our family we are practicing acceptance for one another, when similar behavior patterns rise or fall short. Every time I lose my wallet, I now say, "Okay Ashley, this happens, let's keep looking" versus "There you go again losing shit." My husband bought me a large yellow wallet for my birthday to help me. I haven't lost it yet, I just misplaced it a couple times but it was easily found.

Neuro-divergence for me has become a welcoming of compassion and understanding, this is a time of great change we all can be a part of.

In turn you can lend that grace and ease out unto others. We are made of this world together; healing ourselves impacts us all and spreads.

The solutions for this planet won't come from one person or a governing body; it will be a collective inner process that we are all responsible for. I hold immense faith, vision, and heart for what we are capable of, when we decide to own our power.

To conclude, I came up with some helpful messages that really stood out to me throughout our family's grief healing.

1. Find ways to share how you feel. Honest communication between family members helped us recognize our differences.

In the past, I used to get stuck, overthinking how I could communicate best or avoid upsetting someone. Talking with family began, thoughts or feelings would arise, overwhelm me, or trigger emotion that would lead me to react or shut down. It was messy sometimes, but with patience and commitment to heal, I moved through discomfort toward empathy for myself and in time this helped me to understand others. I began taking intentional pauses to notice my own thoughts and feelings while listening. This became key to being able to hold myself while communicating with another.

Honest communication does not have to be perfect because it won't be. Openness and respect for both sides, in my family, helped us clear up what we thought someone meant or wanted.

Communication is a two-way street. Each of us had our own perceptions and desires while listening to each other. Therefore, we had to become open to hearing the other person's truth. This helped us grow mutual respect and authenticity in our relationships.

Listen to one another to understand versus being right. No one has the same perspectives, needs, or desires. How boring would life be if we didn't disagree, think differently, or create our own ideas? That's what makes Earth so unique to come and create with.

When I learned to listen with a filter, I drastically changed my relationships for the better. My filter directs the energy to my center, focuses on my breath and welcomes understanding. Turning inward helped me be with my body as I listened and took responsibility for my views or feelings.

Important to note, this is an ongoing practice. I sometimes forget and can get caught up in emotions especially when I am exhausted, triggered or fixated on my view. The awareness of this tool helped me come back to myself when listening, catch when I'm responding to be right and try to honor other people where they are.

Communication is a huge foundational skill needed for healthy relationships. When we can listen openly to both sides and disagree with respect, there may be a lot less to process emotionally when grief arrives at the door.

2. Grief isn't linear. Most of life isn't linear but we often expect or want it to be.

Nothing in nature has a perfect straight line; it grows in spirals or in stages with bends and turns. Let go of the expectation that our growth must be a one-way street, "I do this, then it's over." We are part of nature; we move forward then backward.

The day of Ryan's funeral, my dad was approached by a woman at their church offering her condolences. She had lost a son three years earlier. My dad asked, "Does the pain ever go away?" She answered, "No, you just learn how to manage it."

Grief and life are part of one another. We try hard to push it away and avoid it, even fear death, but it's inevitable. I learned to live in the ebbs and flows with trust that life is working for me, even if it feels against me. It's just preparing me for what's next, another opportunity, or desire that's waiting for my attention. After this life, from my perspective, we just keep existing and growing our essence.

In our family, when we allowed the ebb and flow of grief to move us, we learned to embrace hurt and hold strong to love. Love shared reminded us that something profound was present. That love can and continues to hold us after our loved ones are gone. We just found new ways to experience the love and learned to cope with the pain, together.

3. Embrace and appreciate each of your moments. Some victories are small while others are large. I believe the big ones come from the culmination of many small choices. Celebrating the small wins is important because we acknowledge our spirit's effort.

It's taken years to truly accept myself. Countless times in my life, I've sat in discomfort and asked, "What's here for me?" or "What can I learn from this?"

I learned that caring and nurturing myself is the balance to giving and receiving, and the foundation of health.

Everyone gets to decide. I encourage you to ask yourself the hard questions, reflect on your purpose and at any moment, remember you can choose again. There are great fears to be faced and some days I choose to sit out until I gain the strength and courage to try again.

Sometimes it took great courage to be real with myself. Taking small doable steps helps me grow an inner rapport with myself. What that looks like for me is talking it out, holding myself in tears, reaching out for help, taking slow long breaths, walking in nature, drinking water consciously, or letting a loved one hold me.

When I look back months or years, I can see the progression of learning. I can celebrate what was born from hard moments and decisions. This in turn, has helped me grow courage to face more challenges.

4. Make time for reflection and rest. I've learned that eight hours of sleep per night, as often as possible, provides me with the most regulation and grounding. I must choose wisely when to stay up late, and when I do, how to use that potent quiet time.

Having a twenty-minute nap during the afternoon gives me extra strength to be present into the evening. When a nap isn't possible or my mind is too busy or loud, I use guided meditations. Even a five-minute meditation can offer enough to experience a difference.

In the past, evenings were often not spent in contemplation or rest. I used TV or external sources to disconnect myself from hard realities. As time went on, it became important for me to return to self reflection. I got to know my habits and cycles and it gave me a better vantage point of the big picture, especially when the kids were asleep, and the house was quiet.

5. Find patience and humility through the grief process. Unrealistic expectations are slow killers of self-esteem because it never feels like we are enough. It also hinders creativity and joy along the way. I used to take myself too seriously, which added extra stress and pressure that hindered my well being.

In a group setting, humility has allowed me to let down expectations to be more than I was. I can't save the world, certainly not in one day. Practicing flexible expectations and allowing growth to be slow, allowed me to organically shift and show up with others.

I practiced patience and humility with my family, so we could rest and care for ourselves and others. When I got in over my head, thinking I must save the world, I turn to humility to ground myself. When I tried to accomplish too much at once, hearing negative self-talk in my head, that was my cue to pause, acknowledge all that I do, and re-organize my expectations.

6. Be open to what's possible, even if you don't see it yet or fully understand. My mom struggled to believe contact with Spirits was real or possible. She didn't understand and couldn't grasp it without seeing or experiencing herself. It was in my twenties when I found a way to tell my parents I heard and saw spirits; she became curious but still didn't believe it.

Once my mom lost her son and found out that he had contacted me, her openness grew. She desperately wanted to connect with her son. This drastically changed our relationship and through her openness, she was able to get to know me in a whole new way that wasn't possible before. She opened herself to experience Ryan's energy in light, while in bed at night. This was a profound experience for her, seeing and sensing her son's spirit. With a closed mind, it may not have been possible.

I believe moving towards goals can be like this. When I see a challenge with possibility, I become open to creative solutions. Nothing is ever certain. We are being challenged to open ourselves up to new thoughts, solutions, desires, and connections.

7. The power of love is vast and cannot be over-stated. I believe as humans, we've had many conditions, beliefs, and limits placed upon us. Perhaps the greatest lesson of all, is to let go of all we think we know and begin exploring new possibilities with curiosity, joy, and humble hearts.

In my experience, connection with other humans—not just loved-ones—was capable of lighting me up with love, moving me to tears and sent shivers down my arms and spine. When I closed my eyes in meditation, I visited colors, spaces beyond the sky or passed loved ones. I felt love that was alive, all around me. It felt so expansive it was overwhelming, and at times, resulted in my human default, to break the connection. I returned to "reality" as I know it or perhaps the conditioned reality. I asked myself was that real.

Is this earth the only reality? Do we really understand the magnitude of love?

Research has been done; physiological evidence is able to explain the healing power of love. When you experience love, hormonal chemicals provide a biological release. I believe these chemicals help us tap into something greater within ourselves.

For example, when someone is pouring their heart out in a group circle, I can feel empathy, connection, and love for that person. It offers me a visceral experience in my body. When it's my turn to share in the circle, I too share from my heart, providing another person connection and inspiration. When we get the opportunity to meet later in a hug or exchange of conversation, we each feel the rise in love and understanding for one another. Those biological chemicals create the possibilities of healing together. How brilliant!

The healing I experienced with Ryan's Spirit, showed me that the physical presence of someone isn't the only way to experience a biological response of love. Ryan reminded me to turn inward towards the deep center where my Spirit lives. This helped me grow my capacity to hold myself and he helped me allow different ways of receiving love.

When humans pass on, I believe their bodies die but their Spirits continue unto the universe. Loosing the physical density of a body, allows the conscious spark of the Spirit to create an invisible link or channel towards us. Making it possible to feel close together in love, even after they are gone.

It took determination to turn inward, explore curiously and be willing to let love in to move me. Balance kept me seeking, learning, and growing as a human. I hope that my story may offer an example of what's possible, normalize struggles and begin a seed of curiosity into deeper parts of your soul.

Our family continues to encourage each other and honor both my brothers who have passed. Through healing loss, our family continues to learn and live differently thanks to them. With gratitude, we remind each other of how precious life is. We celebrate one another. We call each other out on the habits and old views that keep us trapped. We try to live humbly with kindness, while also learning to accept what shows up in being human.

Have courage to ask hard questions.

Let go of what's holding you back.

Be the change you want to see.

Rest and give love.

Embrace change.

Stand for what you believe in.

May kindness connect you with others.

May your feet walk a little lighter every day on this wonderful planet we call Mother Earth.

Thank you and blessings, my friends.

Printed in Canada